CANNABIS SATIVA

The Essential Guide to the World's Finest Marijuana Strains

Edited by S. T. Oner
With an introduction
by Mel Thomas

Volume
3

GREEN CANDY PRESS

Cannabis Sativa:

The Essential Guide to the World's Finest Marijuana Strains, Volume 3

Published by Green Candy Press

San Francisco, CA

Copyright © 2014 Green Candy Press

ISBN 978-1-937866-29-7

Photographs © ACE Seeds, Acumen Genetics, Alpine Seeds, Asturjaya Seeds, AutoFem by Stitch, AutoFem Seeds, BillBerry Farms, BlimBurn Seeds, Bodhi Seeds, Bodhi Seeds, Breeder Garru, Breeder Stitch, Cali Gold Genetics, California Cannetics, CannaVenture Seeds, Centennial Seeds, Dani, David Strange, David Strange, De Sjamaan, Delta 9 Labs, Dinafem Seeds, DoobieDuck, DPG, Dr. GVZ, Dru West, Dutch Passion, Dynasty Seeds, Ed Borg, Emerald Triangle Seeds, Eva Female Seeds, Evil Seeds, Frank, Gage Green Genetics, Gelston Dwight, Gene Yuss, Gooey Breeder, Granddaddy Purp Genetics, Green Born Identity, Green Dream Health Services, Green Haven Genetics, Green House Seed Co., Greenlife Seeds, GreenMan Organics, High Bred Seeds, HortiLab Seed Company, Humboldt Seed Organisation, Illuminati Seeds, Inkognyto, IrieGenetics Colorado, IrieVibe Seeds, Jamaica Seeds, Jeffman, Jin Albrecht, Joint Doctor, Jordan of the Islands, Julian C, K.W. Estes, Kaliman Seeds, Kannabia Seeds, KindReviews.com, Kingdom Organic Seeds, Kiwiseeds, La Mano Negra, La Plata Labs, Lajuanna, Limestone City Seeds, Luis, Malama Aina Seeds, Mandala Seeds, Matt Dylan, Medical Seeds Co., Ministry of Cannabis, MoD, Mr. Nice Seedbank, Natural GanJahnetics, Next Generation Seed Company, Ocanabis, Original Sensible, Owls Production, Philosopher Seeds, Positronics Seeds, Project CBD, RacerX, Red Herring, Reggae Seeds, Resin Seeds, Ringo, Riot Seeds, Ripper Seeds, Roor Seeds, Royal Canadian Marijuana Collective, Royal Queen Seeds, Ry Prichard, Sagarmatha Seeds, Sannie's Seeds, Satindi Seeds, Sensi Seeds, Serious Seeds, SGS, Shaman Genetics, SickMeds Seeds, Snow, SnowHigh Seeds, SoCal Seed Collective, SoHum Seeds, Spliff Seeds, Stitch, Stoney Girl Gardens, Subcool, Sweet Seeds, Tao of Seeds, Team Green Avengers, The Blazing Pistileros, The Bulldog Seeds, The Rev, Tierra Rojo Genetics, Tight Genes, Tom Hill, TreeTown Seeds, Trip Seeds, Tropical Seeds Company, Tropical Seeds Company, Turtle Man, Ultimate Seeds, Ultra Genetics, Underground Originals, Vulkania Seeds, West Coast Masters, World of Seeds.

Cover photo: King Congo is courtesy and Copyright © Tropical Seeds Company

Printed in China by Oceanic Graphic Printing

Sometimes Massively Distributed by P.G.W.

The web addresses referenced and linked in this book were live and correct at the time of the book's publication but may be subject to change.

Dedication

by S.T. Oner

"The revolution is not an apple that falls when it is ripe. You have to make it fall."
— Che Guevara

As always, I dedicate this book to the fine people at NORML and everyone who has fought against the unjust war on this incredible plant. The work that these organizations continue to do has allowed me not only to begin this dedication with a message of hope rather than defeat, but also is quite literally changing the landscape of cannabis legalization in both the medical and recreational fields. For years now they have been the ones making the apple fall, and for this, we will be forever grateful.

Following the success of the first five books in this series, *Cannabis Indica: The Essential Guide to the World's Finest Marijuana Strains, Volumes 1, 2,* and *3,* as well as *Cannabis Sativa: The Essential Guide to the World's Finest Marijuana Strains, Volumes 1* and *2,* I've watched the spread of this series reach to every corner of the globe. I must thank everyone who's bought one of these guides as well as those many, many talented folks whose work exists on these pages.

Once again, without the fantastic breeders, seed companies, and photographers whose work appears on these pages, I would never have been able to accomplish such a mammoth task. This book features breeders from the USA, Canada, Holland, Britain, Spain, Poland, Chile, Switzerland and quite a few other countries which cannot be listed due to certain draconic laws against this most holy of plants.

There are some contributors who wish to remain anonymous, but who deserve recognition and respect nonetheless, as does everyone on the online forums, especially the folks at Breedbay.co.uk, Meduser.ca, Seedfinder.eu, and Riotseeds.nl.

Finally, I must thank the people who inspired me to learn more about this incredible plant; Ed Rosenthal, Jason King, Danny Danko, Mel Thomas, Mel Frank, Greg Green, Grubbycup Stash, K, Jeff Mowta, Matt Mernagh, Nico Escondido, Jorge Cervantes, Dru West, Ry Prichard, Ringo, and The Rev are some big ones, and of course the unforgettable Jack Herer, may he rest in peace. These guys are true trailblazers and their tireless efforts not only set me on my first steps forward on this wonderful journey, but also keep me balanced throughout it. I feel that *Cannabis Sativa, Vol. 3* is a true representation of the variety of cannabis genetics in existence today, and were it not for the hard work and effort of everyone featured in it, it would not exist at all. For this, I say thank you.

Contents

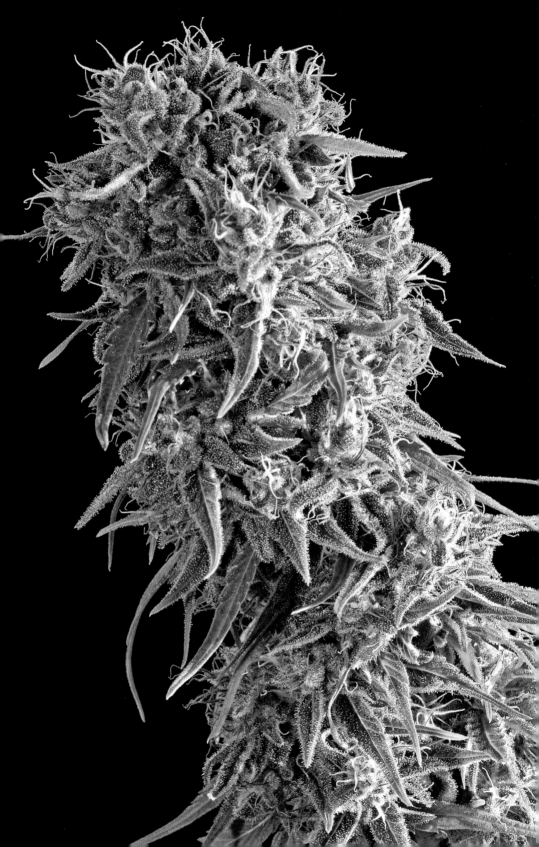

Preface

Cannabis Sativa: Welcome Home

When I first sat down with my meticulously-collected pot samples, blims of hash, little stash baggies, and a large cup of coffee to write *Cannabis Indica: The Essential Guide to the World's Finest Marijuana Strains, Volume 1* back in 2009, I could never have dreamed that, 6 books later, I'd still be sitting here, with an admittedly slightly larger cup of coffee, writing about the best cannabis strains in the world.

To say that the popularity of this series has been a dream come true for me would be an understatement. Thanks to you all buying and enjoying this series, I've been able to showcase strains from some of the best breeders in the world. I've also been able to find out about more different varieties than you could ever imagine—more than I ever thought existed—as breeders and growers from all over the world reached out and told me about their huge new projects, their tiny home grows, and the enigmatic strains that they smoked back in the late 70s that no one ever talks about.

In short, this series has provided me with a marijuana education that I never expected—and it's allowed me to fall in love with sativa strains all over again.

For the last couple of decades, sativa strains have been the second child of the cannabis family. Since the advent of widespread indoor growing, which favored the short stature, hardiness, and heavy yields of indica plants, sativa has been standing behind indica waving its arms and trying to get attention. It's been getting the grades, so to speak, but it slumps away with its bottom lip stuck out when indica keeps getting all the attention.

Of course, there's good reason for this. Many of us simply don't have the grow

Preface

room necessary to cultivate plants that can reach up to 14 feet in height, and very many will reach that height if you turn your back for so much as a minute. Much like the second child, sativa plants can be unruly and difficult to raise, and they're not slow to act out when they don't get the attention they think they deserve. They also love the outdoors and tend to blossom late, meaning that only the most patient of parents can get the best out of them.

When faced with the choice of tall, lanky, and attention-hungry sativa strains or small, chilled out, and easy to grow indicas, most growers began to focus their efforts on indica strains—and others, mostly home growers, didn't even have a choice.

However, while the whole planet was raving about the latest Afghani hybrids and Blueberry strains, sativa lovers were working with their beloved plants to bring them back to the forefront of the growing (and smoking) world. By breeding Haze plants with indicas and Colombian landraces with a variety of Kush strains, the best growers began to make sativa strains more accessible to the general public by bringing their heights down, their yields up, and making them a lot easier to deal with, even for the newbie cultivator.

But not everyone was dedicated to bringing sativa strains indoors; far from it. In fact, the sativa purists out there were more than happy with outdoor growing, and loved that their patience was put to the test with 14-week flowering times and plants so tall that they had to get on a ladder to trim them. But these breeders didn't rest on their laurels either; in fact, they got to work seeking out landrace sativas from all over the world, and to stabilizing the best sativa strains from across the globe.

In short, whilst the vast majority of tokers were looking towards the indica family, the sativa family was quietly blossoming in its own way. Even though sativas enjoyed a relatively quiet popularity, and mainly among old growers from the 70s, magical

things were happening behind the scenes.

With the legal systems of many countries shifting away from prohibition and towards a more progressive, medical-based drugs policy, medical marijuana meant that growers who'd had to hide away in their closets and tiny grow spaces were now able to come out into the open, literally, and to branch out (if you'll pardon the pun) beyond the 4-foot indicas and auto-flowers that they'd come to rely on. Buyers, too, were able to move beyond whatever their black market dealers deigned to throw their way, stating only that they had some "killer kush" that week, and could interact with experts who recommended strains to suit their needs and tastes. With the opening of the first dispensaries, many medical marijuana users realized that they'd been smoking the wrong variety altogether, and numbing themselves with indicas when they really needed something to give them a kick of energy and inspiration. In other words, people finally turned back to sativas—and when the world came a-knocking, sativas were ready.

This book serves as a guide to just how far sativas have come.

Strains like Satori from Mandala Seeds and Chunky Cherry Malawi from The Rev's Kingdom Organic Seeds show the fantastic work that's been done with strains native to far-flung places like Nepal and east Africa. Years ago, U.S. breeders had to make do with Hawaiian and Colombian genetics and, fantastic though those genetics were, they longed for better access to sativa strains. Now, breeders in North America can expand on the amazing breeding that's being done in places like Africa and Asia, and the growing world is much richer for it.

Strains such as Y Griega from Medical Seeds Co. and Amnesika 2.0 from Philosopher Seeds highlight the ever-growing cannabis scene in Spain, Europe's hotbed of marijuana activity right now. With a climate that suits sativa growing down to the ground,

Preface

the south of Spain has embraced outdoor sativa growing and provides some of the best sativa genetics around. Spanish breeders are also proving to be particularly skilled at bringing the best of indica strains into their sativa plants, meaning that the yields are higher and the flowering times shorter.

However, in North America, breeders are also engaged in a project to bring the two varieties together. Their focus, however, has been on bringing sativa traits into indica plants, meaning that hybrids will be small enough to be grown indoors but will have all the psychedelic and head highs that we've come to expect from the best sativa strains. Plants like Jack the Ripper from Subcool's TGA Genetics, and Psycho Killer Bubba Kush from Riot Seeds are opening up the world of sativa strains to those home growers who don't have the space nor the opportunity to grow outdoors, thus bringing the best of sativa to a whole new generation of growers and tokers.

Of course, it's not just the psychedelic highs and the growing traits that define sativa plants. Ask any of your weed-loving grandparents what characterized the best strains of their youth, and they'll undoubtedly mention the delicious tastes of the cannabis from "back in their day." Sativa strains are famous for their fruity smells and berry flavors, and varieties like Dragon's Teeth from Acumen Genetics and Mango Haze from Mr. Nice Seedbank ensure that we don't forget about how truly scrumptious sativa strains can be.

For me, though, more than anything else, sativas will always be the more inspirational of cannabis plants. When I sit down to write to you guys like this, it's always a Diesel strain that I pack into my bowl. When I need to get some fire in me to go outside when it's -10 and the snow sits thick on the ground, it's a Haze that I go for. When I need to find my creativity when it's hidden beneath layers of tiredness and apathy, I'll dig into a

landrace African that sets my soul on fire. For me, there's no bad time for a sativa.

When I say that this series of strain guides has made my dreams come true, then, you can see that I'm talking about more than piles of bud and balls of hash as big as your head (although of course, they're the enjoyable parts, too). It's more than the emails I receive from breeders who've been inspired by the plants on these pages. It's even more than the handshakes, joints, and night-long conversations I've enjoyed with growers from all over the globe, discussing the best way to clone a Haze plant and how exactly to get that beautiful purple color to come through when you live in the tropics.

More than any of that, when I say I'm proud of this strain guide series, I'm talking about the opportunity I've been given to be a part of the sativa revolution; to educate about this amazing cannabis variety as well as to be educated about it, and to catalog the amazing work that sativa breeders have been doing for decades now. It's thanks to everyone featured within the pages of this book that sativa strains have come so far, and that they continue to inspire us today.

So sit back, spark up a J of your favorite Haze, and take a scintillating trip through the universe of sativas. There can be no better way to spend an evening.

Introduction

A Sativa-Lover's History of Marijuana on the West Coast

By The Rev

Now this, this is what I'm talking about right here: Cannabis Sativa. My views of this variety of cannabis have evolved significantly over the last four decades that I have been smoking / growing, and if anything, I love them even more. I'm The Rev, the Cultivation Editor for SKUNK Magazine and author of *True Living Organics*: *The Ultimate Guide to Growing All-Natural Marijuana Indoors*. Grab a copy of my book on Amazon.com or your local bookstore or head shop, and get a subscription to SKUNK Magazine so you can keep current on all the latest all-natural growing advice from yours truly.

I have fond memories of many of the classics from yesteryear, like the Panama Red, which I believe DJ Short described best as "the tequila of weed." I couldn't agree more; and bordering on hallucinogenic for sure in her potency and resin profile, per my experiences with her. I haven't seen any real deal Panama Red for a decade plus, like so many of the old greats. Only watered down versions exist in seed form; because if you ever smoked a real deal Panama Red, you wouldn't forget it for the rest of your life, I assure you, much like my own recollections here, the real Panama Red was a showstopper, heh heh…

My old buddy Snowcap (of SnowHigh Seeds) has a real dedication to the great and mighty sativa, and you can find his seeds at Attitude and Breedbay seed banks, and several of his sativa offerings are in this guide. I got some of Mandala Seeds' Satori—about 2004—and I really loved her, a lot. The first time I smoked the Satori it hit me like Durban Poison with that "rollercoaster" ride with smiles for miles and miles. I see Doobie Duck has some sativa in this book, as well, and I recently saw some of

Introduction

his wares in a recent issue of SKUNK and they sure looked good, mmmmm, Swazi!

There are very few sativas I don't like, or, I should say, they would be my last choice in an array of various sativas to smoke; and not because they are not potent or tasty, but because I don't care for the resin profile, A.K.A. the high-type. One of these is the Humboldt Trainwreck and the Arcata Lemonwreck, which I believe are one and the same as the Lemonwreck may have expressed a "sport" mutation bringing the lemon side out more prominently. The high is aggravating to me during and after the bake. Especially when I come down I tend to be in a bad mood or something. But I'm a weirdo, and most peeps really like the Trainwreck; and she sure does pack a punch!

Before any indoor cannabis breeding (as far as I know) was going on, way back in the late 70s and early 80s, all the breeding was done outdoors. This was problematic for cash croppers who only wanted a few plants pollinated. Prevailing winds and a good distance used to work for us and many like us, just using a remote and somewhat isolated patch for keeping male plants and letting them spew pollen downwind towards the female plants. Since there was limited space, several female varieties were often used, as well as several male varieties. The first generation seeds that came from these pollinations were called the "Trainwreck" generation, since it was a "train wreck" of all killer genetics: you couldn't be sure who pollinated who. After these seeds were grown out, cloned, and inbred they just got names, and different lines from these "train wrecks" of genetics were born. Sometimes they kept the "Trainwreck" in their names, like Humboldt, Purple, L.A., and there were African and Colombian Trainwrecks as well, Mexican and Hawaiian, etc. You get the picture, yes?

I have always been a huge fan of the South East Asian sativa varieties, Thai, Haze, Vietnam Black, and Cambodian, etc. When I was young and learning about outdoor growing and breeding from my buddies, they coveted the South East Asians and the South Africans above all others, with the big exception of the real deal Panama Red, which was everyone's favorite when it was available. Back in the early 80s the real deal Panama Red clone went for $5,000 or so, if that tells you anything. I never even heard the word "Haze" until the mid 80s, and when I smoked some, I instantly recognized it as a South East Asian with an intense and wicked powerful high.

I love the exotic sativas; Congo, Swazi, Malawi, Oaxacan, Colombian, Central and South American varieties, Durban Poison, and some of the old Hawaiians, like the old school Puna Budder, too. Vietnamese genetics also have a special place in my heart. There is nothing quite like them, in my opinion – wow!

Now, here's what I think the big problems are where sativas are concerned. There are many who don't like them, and I think this is why: First and foremost, they flower for a long time, and 14 or 16 weeks flowering is just a ridiculous notion for many. Also, sativas and indicas, using a canine metaphor, are like the wolves (sativas) and the domesticated dogs (indicas). It takes a lot of skills to pull off a 16-week flowering sativa well indoors, period. So, when some peeps try and grow them, they screw up, and the final haul is sub-par at best, if not downright ragweed.

Start out with hybrids first, and I would always want to grow any sativa all natural / organically because of the wolf comparison above. These are wild-ish and highly adaptable plants, and by their very nature don't really like being force fed synthetic nutrients, and it shows. But, smoke some of the sativa that I (or someone who knows how to grow a sativa) grow, and it will change your tune about sativas, I dare say.

One of my very earliest memories regarding sativas, was when I was about 12 years old in the 70s. My friend's cousin was in a pit crew for Modern Motors in the Baja 500 off road race, and many of the crew brought along family and friends. About 7 or 8 of us guests got together in a little "pack" and got into trouble as per usual for rowdy kids. My friend had scored us some "Oaxacan" for $10 U.S., and it was three buds all seeded up; about a quarter ounce per bud, in Ensenada, Mexico. At the same time I was busy getting us a bottle of vodka—no label at all, just a small plastic bear on a chain around the neck of the bottle, and the guy actually sold it to ME. The first night out in the wilderness of Ensenada, about 5 of us wandered off into the dark with sodas—for mixing with the vodka—and this massive red haired sativa. My buddy rolled what we called a "McLendo's Blimp" which was this three paper FAT bomber doobie and we all smoked it while drinking our vodka.

Needless to say we got very high and intoxicated. While trying to walk back to camp I took a fall down into a stream about waist deep with 10 foot sandstone walls on either side. We got so busted by the parents, but it wasn't a giant deal; the giant deal was the next 2 hours or so I spent pulling leeches and ticks off my bad ass wasted self, heh heh.

One of my latest memories was here in my state, Oregon, about a decade ago. Shortly after I arrived, I lost my beloved Vietnam Black (jungle landrace sativa) clone to the cops. I lucked out because I proved that I was in the process of getting my card to be legal, so I didn't go to jail, but they took and killed all of my plants. One of the cops was very impressed with my grow, saying to me: "Ya know what buddy ... If World War III ever starts up I'll be looking you up to grow the food; I have all the guns

Introduction

we'll need." Still makes me smile when I think of that. But I will miss my 16-week flowering Vietnam Black clone forevermore.

Now back when I was just an outdoor sativa grower (Red Bud) before the influx of the Afghanistan Hashplant Indicas (Killer Green Bud) in Northern Cali, the longer flowering time issue had already been dealt with by the more elite outdoor fellas by using some Durban Poison (brought to my mentors via pro surfers of the day) and making Durban Poison hybrids. Now, the "magic" of the Durban Poison is where she is indigenous to: Durban, South Africa, which is about 30 degrees south latitude. In the northern hemisphere she will start flowering outdoors in late June and will finish in the second half of September—BOOM—before any of the coastal funk or rain ever hits. It is a beautiful thing and a trait which stays very dominant in hybrids.

My little trip down memory lane wouldn't be complete without mentioning the Brazilian White Sativa. She also hails from down around 30 degrees south latitude (South American) and shares those photoperiod / early finishing traits of the Durban Poison when grown in the northern hemisphere. She was a favorite clone from the early 80s in Cali for outdoors. She was the (major) mother of many fine lines of cannabis, including the legendary White Widow, I'm pretty stinking sure. The potency of this Brazilian clone was close to the Panama Red, not quite the 6 hour ride of Panama Red, but damn outstanding, for sure.

When I left Northern Cali and headed back down to SoCal, I took several killer clones with me, including Durban Poison. The first season I got back I took 20 Durban Poison clones and planted them next to a flood control channel near a place called Mission Valley in San Diego. They got good runoff water from a hill on one side of the channel and were low in a valley so the natural water table stayed pretty available.

I would take bike rides and check on them, and they were scattered along about a half mile of the channel; they were very camouflaged and you would have to be hunting there for cannabis or know they were there to even see them. Two or three of my close buddies knew about the plants, and I had enlisted them to help me harvest them when they were done for some of the herbs.

So, it's like three days from harvest, about 6 am, and I get a call from one of my friends telling me he saw two California Department of Transportation trucks going into the channel when he drove by. I grabbed a big duffle bag and a large ass backpack and launched on my mountain bike. It was about a 40-minute ride and when I arrived I saw one truck and two guys in orange vests right up next to a couple plants

Introduction

definitely knowing what they were because Man they looked and smelled good.

I almost bailed, but didn't for some reason. Instead, I waited and watched from a canyon entrance a bit above the scene. After about 15 minutes they took off, but in my heart I knew they would be returning. I hauled ass down and started a maniac harvest session, just cramming the branches into my duffle bag and backpack as I went from plant to plant only taking the most apical branches with the largest buds and leaving the rest of the plants still in the ground. I had enough room for a lot, but not all; and the smell, good gawd!

Now I only had a 40-minute bike ride and I would be home, and I knew the flowers would still be fine as long as I got them out of the bag and backpack within an hour or so. It was about 8 am or so, and I opted to take a little shortcut right through the Mission Valley Mall; a huge mall, nothing was really open yet there, and it would take about 10 minutes off my time, which was uber important if I was going to save the flowers.

I took off, and as I crossed the intersection just before entering the mall proper I zipped by a few cute girls crossing the street; within 10 seconds of me passing them, they were yelling they loved me and to please come back! Yep, I was THAT stinky; in a good, dank way. While hauling ass through the mall I could look back and always see peeps looking at me, no doubt enveloped by my dank-scented trail of smells.

So far so good, but then I hit a trashcan and it pissed off a beehive apparently because looking back I saw the swarm on my ass—bees can't quite catch a mountain bike at full speed by the way, but they can come damn close! A guy opened the door to one shop and saw me (and the bees) and told me to hurry up and come inside, so I did. His next words were: "Damn dude!" He was just blown away by the stench as I went out the back door, heh heh. I made it home and the flowers turned out killer. I went back the next day and all the plants had been removed from the flood control channel gardens—whew!

You really should try some killer sativa herbs sometime; it just might be the ticket you've been looking for. With more growers and consumers becoming savvy, I am sure sativas and sativa-dominant hybrids will get more attention because the facets are endless: the flavors, resin profiles, etc. I love sativas, and I have a little seed company called Kingdom Organic Seeds (KOS) which has a bunch of killer sativas and sativa hybrids; available online at Hemp Depot.

Cheers amigos, and enjoy this excellent bunch of sativas and sativa hybrids in this edition of *Cannabis Sativa*: *The Essential Guide*!

CANNABIS
SATIVA
The Strains

Acapulco Gold

I don't know much about Acapulco, although I gather that you can begin to have myriad mental health issues if you stay too long. Clearly, SnowHigh knows more about this beautiful Mexican city than me, as he has selected an Heirloom Sativa from the region for his version of this gorgeous strain that's been called the best in the world. Acapulco Gold is certainly not for the faint of heart, whether you're smoking or growing. As you would expect from an Heirloom Sativa, there's a lot of wildness in this strain and inexperienced cultivators will most likely find it to be more than they can handle. However, it's not too tall and should finish after around 70 days of flowering, which generally translates to about mid-October when grown outdoors. This plant will flourish in the great wide open, grown in good quality soil, and the purists among us will say that an organic soil grow is the only way to go. This strain deserves respect and attention, and she'll reward you greatly if you give that to her.

After the taste of burnt sugar subsides, hang on to your hat. This strain throws you into a racecar and steps on the gas. If you're not seeing things, hearing voices, or seeing the world in a blur, then you're a stronger person than me. By the end of it, I was definitely going loco.

SnowHigh Seeds, USA

Heirloom Mexican Sativa

Genetics: Mexican Sativa

Amnesia Haze

Holland's Royal Queen Seeds have got their hands on a killer strain with this one. If you've not heard of Amnesia Haze before you've either been in some sort of tragic coma for the last 20 years or you've been living in one of those cults where people aren't allowed to speak to people from the outside world—and in both cases, let me take this time to say welcome back to reality. The rest of us, however, already know that Amnesia Haze is a super popular mix of Amnesia, Skunk, and Haze genetics that gives a gorgeously heady high and an interesting brain effect that's unlike any other. The Royal Queen Seeds boys have their own unique version of this wonderful plant, and it's definitely worth taking notice of.

Amnesia Haze can grow up to 6 feet and beyond if allowed, so indoor growers may have to engage in some Low Stress Training to ensure that their crops don't grow too big and wild. Whilst this strain is really made for indoor growing, cultivators in hotter places like Australia, Africa, or Central America should be able to find some success outside, while even Californian tokers should be able to get a good amount of bud from this plant. Outdoor growers should be aware, however, that Amnesia Haze is a fairly sensitive plant, so extra care will need to be taken against inclement weather, pests, mold, and other potential irritants. If you can protect your crops from the elements sufficiently you'll be rewarded eventually with a stronger harvest and a truly fantastic plant. Indoor growers should pack as much light into their grow rooms as physically possible, as this will ensure the heaviest yield possible. Suitable for both organic and hydro grows, this is a relatively simple plant indoors, although growers should always watch out for the beginnings of mold. After the relatively long 12-week flowering period indoor growers should be able to bring in around 600 grams of bud per square yard of grow room under 600 watts of light. Outdoors in good conditions, this strain can produce up to 200 grams per plant.

Royal Queen Seeds,
Holland
Sativa-Dominant
Genetics: Amnesia Haze
Potency: THC 19%
royalqueenseeds.com

The Royal Queen Seeds breeders recommend giving your harvested buds at least 2 weeks of curing to really bring out the flavor, and you won't be sad that you followed their advice when you're breathing in the fresh, fruity smoke and feeling the tangy sweetness play across your tongue. Be warned, though, that this light flavor gives way to an incredible head high, the type that leaves you unaware of your surroundings and incapable of remembering your own name. Even veteran smokers will find that a full joint or a super large bong hit really will put them in an Amnesia Haze.

Amnesika 2.0

Spain's Philosopher Seeds are well known in their native Europe, and with this Amnesika 2.0 strain it's not hard to see why. A combination of genetics from three different stellar strains, Amnesika 2.0 can count Super Silver Haze, G-13 Haze and Skunk amongst its family members.

Despite being sativa-dominant, this is a plant that's well versed in how to properly grow indoors and won't even pose too many challenges for a fairly inexperienced grower. The breeders recommend cultivating this strain indoors in 2 gallon pots, with a density of up to 12 plants per square yard of grow space, although 3 gallon pots with more space per plant can also be a great set up. Prune her at the 5th internode, and allow for 3 weeks of vegetative growing. If grown outdoors this plant can easily reach 6 feet and above, and it will be ready for harvest around the first two weeks of October. After 65 days of flowering indoors you can take down 450 grams per square yard, and the same amount from one plant outdoors.

**Philosopher Seeds,
Spain**

Sativa-Dominant

Genetics: Super Silver x
G-13 Haze x Skunk

Potency: THC 16-18%

philosopherseeds.com

This is a smoke that tastes like roasted hazelnuts and cold coffee with a hint of that sweet Skunk, too. The high brings on a great mood and puts a spring in your step as well as making you concentrate beautifully. A great strain for introspection and appreciation of art.

Angelmatic (AKA Little Angel)

Look guys, Holland's Ministry of Cannabis might have acres of grow space and the ability to grow all the marijuana they could ever want, but they weren't always one of Europe's most well-known seed banks. They understand that you might only have a really tiny grow room or a closet in which to grow your pot; they've been there. Once upon a time they were teenagers growing out of their spare rooms and closets—and now they want to help you out. In fact, they specifically want you to be able to grow sativa-dominant hybrids even if your grow space is smaller than your average fridge. They believe you can do it, and that's why they created Angelmatic, otherwise known as Little Angel.

By crossing a Little Devil plant with a Ruderalis variety, Ministry of Cannabis have brought auto-flowering characteristics to an already great plant. This means that the plant will mature fully in a short amount of time regardless of the amount of light she's subjected to. It also means she will only grow about a foot in height and therefore can be grown very easily in very little space. This kind of strain is a Godsend for the rookie grower, and especially for light medical marijuana users who don't need an excessive amount of bud but would like to grow their own. Angelmatic isn't a high yielder but will bring in a harvest very quickly and easily, meaning that for those who need a little pain relief after work and want to have some homegrown stash, this plant is near perfect. Little Angel will start to flower about 2.5 weeks after germination, and the whole thing will be done, dusted, and leaving for college with your car 60 days from seed. She won't ever get too stinky, meaning that you shouldn't have to bother with charcoal filters or other odor-defying methods. If you'd like to use a SOG method you can, and this crop will be resistant to pests and won't need much more than good soil and a generous supplement of nitrogen. Indoors, from small plants, you can expect to harvest about 50 grams of bud from each one. Outdoors, however, your plants can grow taller and wider as well as having easier access to more light, so you might find yourself with slightly bigger plants that yield up to 100 grams in full summer in a temperate climate.

Ministry of Cannabis, Holland

Auto-Flowering

Sativa-Dominant

Genetics: Ruderalis x Little Devil

Potency: THC 12-15%

ministryofcannabis.com

Your Angelic little buds will be like medium-sized green cones, and will smell like fresh flowers and sour bubblegum candy. There's an aftertaste of sourness once the smoke has cleared, and the high is a social and interactive one that isn't very concentrated but, instead, offers a relaxing vibe. Great "after dinner" pot!

Bay 11

You know how excited you got when you realized that that guy who did Gangnam Style didn't just do Gangnam Style, and in fact had a whole K-pop career before that song and also continued to make tunes after? That's about how I felt when I realized that Granddaddy Purp Genetics, the masters behind the incredibly popular Grand Daddy Purp, don't just make that one strain. In fact, this small seed company is putting out some of the most exciting strains in the U.S. right now. Bay 11 is a sativa-dominant bred from secret sources that's already won awards and has captured the attention of the California cannabis community like no other.

Bay 11 is a fantastic medical strain that was developed with the express goal of providing great pain relief for those that need it, when they need it. Indoors, it can be constrained to about 4 feet in height, but outdoors it will grow beyond 10 feet if you allow it to—and if you've got the space, I recommend that you let it grow as tall and wild as it wishes. As is the case with the vast majority of sativa-dominant strains, this plant can be a little leggy and will exhibit some stretch if it's deprived of light in a grow room, so if you're an indoor grower, be sure to keep your lamps close to the seedlings, but beware of burning them. These plants are heavy yielders, so be sure to give your plants some good support right from the vegetative stage so they don't bend and snap in flowering. The buds of this plant explode in a riot of color; they're the cannabis equivalent of setting off a bunch of party poppers. Deep green with accents of white and orange and even cheeky hints of blue, these flowers are a joy to behold and will make your grow room look like there's a party going down 24/7. Indoors, you should be ready to go after 9 or 10 weeks of flowering, whereas outdoor growers will need to wait until the end of October before they can go in for the chop. This extra patience, however, will pay dividends; outdoor growers can bring in an absolutely phenomenal 1500 to 2500 grams per plant (I know; it brings me out in a sweat, too) whereas indoor growers will bring in a very respectable 1000 grams per square yard of grow space.

Granddaddy Purp Genetics, USA

Sativa-Dominant

Genetics: Unknown

Sativa

granddaddypurp.com

The sweet and fresh smell of Bay 11 buds are offset by a hint of berries, meaning that smoking this feels like you're chewing fruity gum. This strain, though, isn't really about the taste; it's about the effect. A great daytime smoke, Bay 11 can help with relief of chronic pain as well as appetite disorders and can provide great relief for those suffering from sleep disorders.

Blue City Diesel

Diesel fans, rejoice, because there can never be too many awesome Diesel crosses, and Blue City Diesel is certainly one of them. Bred by the awesomely named Jordan of the Islands from Canada and grown by the incredibly talented West Coast Masters, this strain comprises West Coast Blueberry genetics as well as New York City Diesel genes. On paper it sounds great, and in real life it's even better.

Blue City Diesel grows to between 4 and 6 feet (even when when grown outdoors), making it a great strain for indoor cultivation, and the tough, hardy nature of these plants means they can handle almost anything—even stupid rookie errors. The breeder recommends growing in a ScrOG set up with organic nutes for best results. These beautiful blue-tinged foxtailing buds are like works of art, but don't hesitate to chop the hell out of them once the very short 55 day flowering period is over, as they'll be better in your bowl than in your grow room. Expect a heavy harvest, and remember to control the crazy strong odor in the later stages of flowering.

This strain tastes like a fresh blueberry muffin straight out of the oven, and the high will warm your insides just as a muffin would. Medicinal users will love this strain for its pain-killing properties, while the rest of us can enjoy its balanced, positive, uplifting high.

Bred by Jordan of the Islands, Canada and grown by the West Coast Masters, USA

Sativa-Dominant

Genetics: West Coast Blueberry x New York City Diesel

Potency: THC 22.5%

jordanoftheislands.ca

westcoastmasters.com

Bruce Banner

Alright, all you comic book geeks form an orderly line behind this nerdlinger here, because I will fight you all to get my hands on this strain if I really need to. Obviously named after the genius alter ego of the somewhat unpredictable Hulk, this strain from America's Green Dream Health Services is an alluring mix of Strawberry Diesel and Ghost OG genetics that will have Marvel fans foaming at the mouth.

There are 5 different phenotypes expressed by this plant; the one pictured to the right is the Bruce 3 pheno, considered by the breeders to be the most perfectly balanced mix of Diesel and OG genetics in the whole crop. This is the most potent overall, although all buds tested very highly even when grown by rookie cultivators, meaning that it's a great strain to try if this is your first grow. As the purple hues on your plants emerge, they'll look less like the big green guy and more like pretty flowers that won't smash a God into the floor repeatedly.

The smoke, though, will smash you into the ground—but not after an incredibly hectic, energetic high that lasts for a few hours and might be a bit much for some people. Some people ask me why this high doesn't seem to affect me so much. My response? "That's my secret, Captain. I'm always high."

Green Dream Health Services, USA

Sativa-Dominant

Genetics: Strawberry Diesel x Ghost OG

Potency: THC 20%

greendreamhealth.com

Bubba Sativa (AKA Wicked Bubba, Orgnkid's Sativa Pheno)

No, this isn't the name of Boba Fett's stoner twin brother; this is a Riot Seeds cross between Wicked Bubba and Orgnkid's Sativa Pheno of everyone's favorite: Bubba Kush. Kush lovers who want to explore a little outside their comfort zone will absolutely love this innovative cross!

Medium height with thin, deep green leaves, and long, slightly loose buds, Bubba Sativa is a gorgeous plant to grow and smoke. She is mostly green and yellow colored for the 10-week flowering period. The production of this line has been greatly improved with this strain, meaning that you should be able to harvest up to 650 grams of prime bud per square yard of grow space.

With tell-tale taste of the Bubba Kush coming through in the smoke, this strain will trick you into thinking that the high is going to be typical. Don't be fooled: it isn't. This strain gives the type of high that encompasses both head and body, being buzzy and thrilling as well as sedate and trippy. Although any sensible stoner will be excited by this plant, medical users will truly appreciate its ability to combat depression, nausea, and chronic pain.

PHOTOS BY RACERX

Riot Seeds, USA

Sativa-Dominant

Genetics: Orgnkid's Bubba Kush Sativa Pheno x Wicked Bubba

Potency: THC 17-19%

riotseeds.nl

Chemdawg

The story of Chemdawg has been told a million times, each version slightly different from the next, but let's go over the legend one more time to help the newbies catch up. The story goes that the original breeder of this strain, Chemdog, met up with a dude called Joe at a Grateful Dead concert and bought from him an ounce of high quality pot for $500. They exchanged numbers, and Chemdog later bought two more ounces from Joe. Legend tells us that when those ounces reached Chemdog on the East Coast, one ounce was seedless and the other was not, containing 13 of the cannabis equivalent of magical beans. In 1991, Chemdog finally popped those beans, and they gave rise to the whole family of ChemDawgs. Some speculate that the genetics were an unknown indica, whilst others have guessed at Nepalese and Thai parentage. We just don't know. What we do know, however, is that ChemDawg is a true classic, and Humboldt Seed Organisation has refined it to the point of perfection with this release. It is amazing.

Your ChemDawg seeds should pop fairly quickly, even under 24 hours in some cases. This vigor will stay with the plants throughout all the vegetative stage, and if you're not careful this can translate into some unwanted stretch. This shouldn't be an issue for outdoor growers, but if you're short on indoor grow space you want to stunt the height as much as possible, which can pose a challenge. In fact, this strain is not generally recommended for rookie growers as it can present a whole host of challenges that only an experienced cultivator would know how to deal with. As a fairly balanced sativa dominant strain, ChemDawg exhibits medium to thick leaves with a gorgeous deep green color. At about day 40 of the vegetative stage you'll want to flip them into flower and you'll also want to check your plants for any sign of nutrient burn; this strain doesn't like to be overfed with anything and will definitely let you know if she's had too much. Outdoors, growers should be ready for harvest at around the first week of October, while indoor growers should let their ChemDawg crop go for around 9 weeks after forced flowering. Indoors, the yield will be moderate, but outdoors it can spill over into above average.

Your finished ChemDawg buds will be utterly delicious looking; the sort of nugs that have 20-year-old stoners oohing and aahing like they've just seen a newborn puppy. With a piney, fuel smell, these buds will get you higher than a kite with cut strings and happier than a pig in a pile of fresh shit.

Humboldt Seed Organisation, USA

Sativa-Dominant

Genetics: Unknown bagseed

Potency: THC 20%

humboldtseeds.co.uk

Chemdog x Amnesia

Ultimate Seeds certainly know what's hot and what's not in the world of pot (I'm a poet and I didn't even realize it!). To create this sativa-dominant hybrid they've combined two of the most popular strains of the last two decades. An indica-heavy Chemdog IX-III and an Amnesia plant come together to make this strain that's only a little more sativa than indica, meaning that along with hybrid vigor and a great high this strain has traits that indoor growers will love.

The structure of this plant might be different to ones you've seen before, as the indica and sativa sides of the equation fight it out to decide which one is king of the grow room. Chemdog x Amnesia won't grow so tall that it becomes a problem, but it will still be fairly leggy and will jump at any chance to stretch. I suggest you invest some time in training and keep your lights hung low. Outdoors, let her grow: your yield will thank you for it. After a medium-long 10 week flowering period you should be ready to bring in an above average harvest, but this plant is more about quality than it is about quantity.

Ultimate Seeds

Sativa-Dominant

Genetics: Chemdog IX-III x Amnesia

Potency: THC 22%

ultimateseeds.com

When you eventually spark up your homegrown buds from this strain, set yourself in for a nice long experience as this high is one that simply won't let go. You'll be soaring above the clouds for hours and hours, paranoia-free and flying on a cloud of delicious spicy smoke.

Choke Berry

The Blazing Pistileros are a favorite company of mine, because they exhibit their crazy skills with humor and grace, and to see that they're using genetics from Loompa for this strain brings tears of joy to my red eyes. By combining the Pistileros' famous Mau-Mau with a Moondawg from Loompa's Farm, they were always going to court some attention, but by naming the plant for my favorite old-time rock n' roller, they've made me want to kiss their damn faces.

Choke Berry plants will grow with lots of side branching and a generally bushy structure, so when they're Almost Grown they'll look more like indicas than sativas. Whether you grow indoors or outdoors under the Little Stars, your plants will need a lot more than Thirty Days to finish; in fact, they'll need 75. You better hope that when the harvest rolls around you've got No Particular Place to Go, as your yields will be around 600 grams per square yard, meaning there's a lot of work to do. After a hard day's harvesting, you'll be Too Pooped to Pop!

Depending on the phenotype you get, your Choke Berry high might leave you Feelin' It in the body, or you might be all Go-Go-Go. Whichever you get, my advice is to get yourself a Good Lookin' Woman and dance all the way From St. Louie to Frisco.

IrieVibe Seeds featuring The Blazing Pistileros, Spain

Sativa-Dominant

Genetics: Loompa's Moondawg x Mau-Mau

Potency: THC 18% / CBD 1.20%

irievibeseeds.com

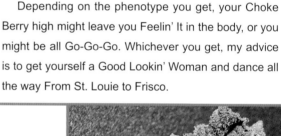

Chunky Cherry Malawi

The USA's Kingdom Organic Seeds is the seed company of the Rev, SKUNK Magazine's resident cultivation expert and author of True Living Organics, his book on how to grow like a mad boss without the use of any synthetics. If that doesn't convince you that he knows what he's talking about, consider that this strain is a three-way F1 hybrid between Deep Chunk, the plant that yields like it's a million feet tall, and a delicious Cherry Malawi. Crazy, right?

Cherry Malawi's parents are some of the dankest sativas to come out of Africa's southern regions, so expect Chunky Cherry Malawi to have inherited at least some of those awesome traits. The indica in the Deep Chunk has tamed this plant a lot, meaning that it can be grown indoors as well as out and will yield dense, fat buds even though its leaves are pale yellow and thin. Although the yields won't be as huge as a Deep Chunk stash, at the end of the 50-60 day flowering period you should take home a medium-heavy harvest of nugs that smell like Cherry Cola and will kick you right into the air.

Kingdom Organic Seeds by The Rev, USA

Sativa-Dominant

Genetics: Deep Chunk x Cherry Malawi

facebook.com/
  KingdomOrganicSeeds
facebook.com/
  TrueLivingOrganics

Sugary, resinous, and smelling like candy, these buds promise to be delicious—and they are. The energetic, balanced high is just as enjoyable, and makes for a great daytime smoke when you need a bit of help over hump day.

Chupacabra

Spain's SickMeds Seeds' Chupacabra (which I swear to God means "suck a goat", but what does my shaky Spanish know?) is a resinous beast that is 70% sativa and helps with stress and muscular pain. Sharing the shame mother as SickMeds The Wreck and their Strawberry Fire, this is a beautiful strain that gives a very psychedelic sativa high.

There's a whole lot of sativa influence in these plants, so expect your Chupacabra crop to be tall and gangly. They'll almost definitely have to be trained, although if you prepare for this early on it won't be too much work. You won't find your crop ravaged by mold or pests, and they also won't be too demanding in the way of nutrients. By the end of the 60-70 day flowering period (dependent on grow style) your plants will be ready for the chop; this should be the last week of October if you're growing outdoors. Expect something like 550 grams per square yard of grow space.

Chupacabra buds smell dankier than Kush but not as stinky as Cheese, with tones of incense and, when busted, a nice, fresh smell of citrus. This is an incredibly clear and focused high that will get shit done for you without any paranoia. Perfect for a cheeky toke before work or in the middle of class during the break!

SickMeds Seeds, Spain

Sativa-Dominant

Genetics: Trainwreck IBL BCO x Strawberry Fire

Potency: THC 17.9%

sickmeds.com

Colombian Gold

The USA's Gage Green Genetics have gone to the land of the neverending siesta for this strain, a fantastic pure sativa bred from a landrace Colombian plant that grows freely in the fields over there. The Gage Green breeders jumped at the chance to work with such quality genetics, and this strain shows that they certainly did the seeds justice.

As with any landrace strains, Colombian can be challenging for newbie growers, towering as it does above many other sativas, growing thin and lanky with a hell of a lot of stretch. This isn't the tallest strain you'll ever see, but it's definitely more of an outdoor strain than an indoor. Plants will need to be staked in the vegetative stage to offer support when their heavy, loose buds start to come in, and as the flowering stage can often last into the fourth month and even beyond, Colombian growers better have a truck load of patience and more than a little skill. Your yield will be medium heavy, but the thick aroma of perfume will convince you that these buds are all class.

Gage Green Genetics, USA

Pure Sativa

Genetics: Landrace Colombian Sativa

Potency: THC 12%

gagegreen.org

This is the pot that made the 60s and 70s so special; a soaring 5-hour high that will change your whole life if you let it. Treasure the seeds of Colombian if you can get them, as this is pot that you don't find very often.

CookieWreck

Named after what I look like after the munchies hit at 4am and I try to cram an entire box of Chips Ahoy! in my mouth, this strain from America's CannaVenture Seeds is a cross between the popular Arcata Trainwreck BX II and Girl Scout Cookies—the plant, not the tasty tasty treat.

This sativa-dominant strain grows tall and thin and works just as well indoors as outdoors. It has two phenos: a Trainwreck pheno with big yield, and a less heavy Girl Scout Cookies pheno that produces gorgeous looking bud. The latter tends to exhibit more interesting colors and can also be more fragrant, but ultimately your favorite is going to be dictated by whether or not you're growing for the biggest yields. Both types are something to write home about, and with either one you're looking at an above-average yield in just under 10 weeks of flowering. Be sure to give your freshly-cut buds a nice long curing period to draw out the best flavors and smells, and when they emerge, be sure to appreciate the beautiful purple tones as well as the wicked smell.

The heavy trichome production of CookieWreck means it's a good choice for hash production, but regardless of how you choose to consume, you'll enjoy a nice lemony sweet smoke and a heady high that comes with enough body buzz to keep you relaxed.

PHOTOS BY DR. GVZ

CannaVenture Seeds, USA

Sativa-Dominant

Genetics: Girl Scout Cookies x Arcata Trainwreck BX II

Potency: THC 18.97% / CBD 1.91%

cannabis-seeds-bank.co.uk

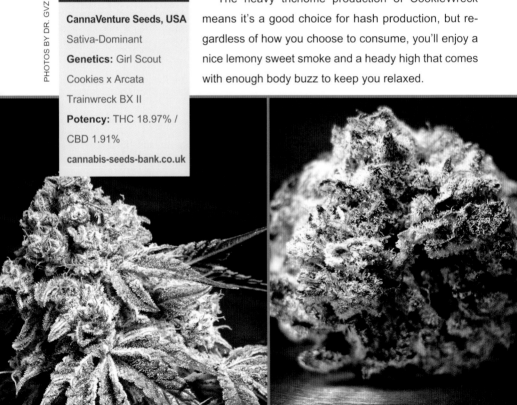

Critical Haze

Spain's Resin Seeds are a great seedbank hailing from Barcelona, where founder Jaime opened one of the first grow shops in Spain back in the day. Active since the late 90s, the guys and girls over at Resin have honed their craft over many years and are now known as experts in the field, speaking at events and participating in breeders' projects all over Europe. In short, the kids at Resin Seeds know what they like: they like sativa strains that yield like the thickest, fattest indica but retain all the best traits of both types of pot. They also know how to get exactly that: by crossing a stellar sativa with a high-yielding indica and working with it until it's perfect. To this end, Resin Seeds present Critical Haze to the world. This strain counts a reverted Amnesia Haze (the HP one, not Soma's) and a female clone of Critical Mass as its parent strains, and it is a near-perfect marriage of sativa highs and indica yields. Job done, guys. Job done.

The Critical Mass parent of Critical Haze was a particularly vigorous plant, so you can expect the same from your Critical Haze crops right from the very beginning. As this strain is only just sativa-dominant, you can expect the plants to grow medium tall and to be quite bushy, certainly a lot bushier than heavier sativa strains that grow incredibly tall and thin. Indoors or outdoors, this strain will be at its best when treated to a large amount of light, so don't be afraid to pack more T5s into your grow room or splash out on that extra HPS bulb. Al-though Critical Haze enjoys a good resistance to pests, you should keep an eye out for mold taking hold as the buds fatten up into full maturity. The colas produced by Critical Haze are beauty in (slow) motion; greener than the brownies that Snoop Dogg made with Martha Stewart that time, they form a spear-like shape with absolutely stunning foxtail buds and by the time they're fully mature that look as if they're made of silky-soft velvet. The tear-shaped serrated leaves fan out from the buds as if presenting them to the Miss Universe judging panel, and after a 10 or 11 week flowering period they'll certainly be the best in show. The fantastic yielding will give you a harvest of at least 500 grams of bud per square yard of grow space, and outdoor growers will take home at least 400 grams per plant.

In keeping the best of the sativa side in this plant, Resin Seeds have made a beast that tastes of Pure Haze, all spice and tang with a slight hint of something sour and fruity underneath. The high is all up there: strong, long lasting and cerebral with just enough body buzz to make it nice and relaxing.

Resin Seeds, Spain

Sativa-Dominant

Genetics: Amnesia Haze x Critical Mass

Potency: THC 18-22%

resinseeds.net

PHOTO BY JULIAN C.

D.T.S.

America's BillBerry Farms aren't the Beyonce of the seed world. They don't release strains to major mainstream acclaim and waltz around demanding the best seats at Willie Nelson shows because they've got all the good pot. Instead, they're like the Pixies in the mid 90s; they plug away doing what they do, being incredibly good at it, and enjoying a small but dedicated fanbase, of which I am most certainly a member.

D.T.S., however, is a strain worthy of mainstream acclaim, thanks to the blending of four different and equally impressive genetic lines: Cheeze, MK-Ultra, Silver Diesel Haze and Head Banger. At anywhere between 2 and 9 feet, D.T.S. is the sort of plant that will happily lay roots wherever you put it, adapting to the situation as it finds it. It's not too fussy about anything in particular, but it does tend towards bushiness, so leave a little room around your seedlings so that they can grow nice and fat. D.T.S. clones like a dream, and if you decide to grow this strain in a Screen of Green set up, it will be happy enough to blossom forth in just 75 days and give you a great yield that smells of earth and citrus.

BillBerry Farms, USA

Sativa-Dominant

Genetics: (Cheeze x MK-Ultra) x (Silver Diesel Haze x Head Banger)

Potency: THC 16%

billberryfarmstissue culture.com

D.T.S. buds will give you a strong, intense head high with a nice body buzz, too. It's perfect weed for kicking back and talking about Lord of the Rings for hours with your buddies.

Dawgtown Daze

Okay, Haze fans. Take a seat. No seriously; I don't want you to fall down and crack your head open when you read the rest of this page. Are you comfortable? Okay; if your cranium is safe then I guess we can talk about this great strain from America's SoCal Seed Collective, bred by California Cannetics. Dawgtown Daze is a combination of genetics from a male ChemDawg plant and a female Pure Haze. Yep; a pure, original Haze. No, don't hyperventilate. Breathe into this bag. It's going to be fine.

If you can get over the excitement of reading that family tree, we should probably talk about how you can grow this thing, too. As a hybrid that's over 90% sativa, this strain is going to grow tall and flower long. It would probably suit outdoor growers best, although it can be grown indoors without too much hassle. Just ensure that you engage in some Low Stress Training to keep it a little bit tamed. Dawgtown Daze has a good amount of stretch in her, so if you're attempting to keep your plants as short as possible, don't put your lights too far from her leaves or you're going to end up with a straggly crop. Anyone who's familiar with Haze cultivation will love seeing the Haze traits come through as this plant matures into a beautiful, blossoming thing— all serrated leaves and deep green hues. As the buds begin to thicken and come in, you'll start to see evidence of some foxtailing which will accelerate as the crop gets towards harvest time. This plant is an above-average yielder, and as it is a skinny, lanky plant, it's important to provide it with support; the earlier, the better. The good news for indoor growers is that even towards the end of flowering, Dawgtown Daze barely has any stink to it, although you shouldn't let that make you complacent; check outside your grow room every day for any escaping evidence of the dank within. There are several different phenotypes expressed by this strain, and although they are very similar, they can differ greatly when it comes to flowering time. Most phenos will be finished after 10 or 12 weeks of flowering, but some won't be fully mature until week 16. Don't rush your plant and let it decide for itself when it's ready for the chop!

With white, green, orange, and even a hint of purple, it's easy to fall head over heels in love with these buds. When you spark them up, that familiar Haze smell will fill the air before taking over your nostrils. The high, of course, is a powerful, soaring one; a long journey through your own soul.

SoCal Seed Collective, USA, breeder California Cannetics

Sativa-Dominant

Genetics: Pure Haze x ChemDawg (Male)

Potency: THC 19.23% / CBD 0.22%

socalseedco.com

Doobie's Malawi

The talented DoobieDuck is a private medical breeder hailing from the U.S., and he's not afraid to work with some rare genetics. In fact, Doobie's Malawi originated as a landrace African Sativa, and, seeing the potential of this beautiful plant, the breeder crossed it with a Massachusetts SuperSkunk x Sour Bubble hybrid from Head Seeds. The resulting plant will have you smiling like a crazy person quicker than you can say "ballin' strain."

The wide spreading traits of the Malawi sativa have been well-tamed by the MSS x SB indica here, resulting in a medium tall plant that can be kept short with good training, although indoor growers will still need a hell of a lot of space. Resistant to mold and only needing very light feeding, Doobie's Malawi nevertheless can have some issues with mites. Halfway through the 90-day flowering period the buds will seriously bulk up, leaving you with a very heavy harvest! This plant grows long colas that tighten up over time, and when it's ready for the chop her buds will be incredibly resinous and so sticky that they catch you like Velcro whenever you brush past.

DoobieDuck, USA

Sativa-Dominant

Genetics: Malawi Gold x (Massachusetts Super-Skunk x Sour Bubble)

doobieduck.com

Doobie's Malawi buds smell like sugar and spice and taste like sweet coffee; a perfect accompaniment to your morning cup of joe. The high is an immediate head and body rush that mellows out into a very creative, productive high. This beauty may be too much for rookie tokers.

PHOTOS BY DOOBIEDUCK

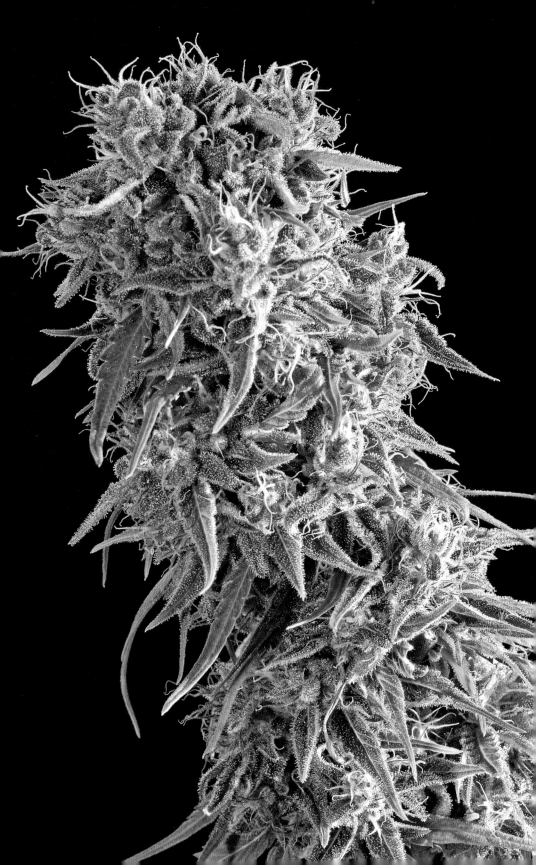

Dragon's Teeth

The USA's Acumen Genetics breed great cannabis and use phenomenal genetics. They are not your average tokers-turned-growers-turned breeders. In fact, founder Gene E. Yuss was a man with a plan , and he eventually brought together experts from a number of different fields, all based in Agricultural Sciences, to create a group of people who could bring differing levels of expertise to the cultivation and breeding of the cannabis plant. Tasking themselves with improving the quality of the seed stock in the U.S., this group of people pooled their genetics and got to work, applying their skills in the most serious way. For Dragon's Teeth, they've crossed a Sativa Spirit mother plant with an exceptional SAGE male, with the hopes that the latter would bring its resistance to pests and its heightened THC to the offspring. They were not disappointed.

With only a 10% indica influence, Dragon's Teeth is a very sativa heavy plant and as such, will grow to around 6 or 8 feet if left untopped. Indoor growers can maintain a small plant by training and topping their plants, but even if this doesn't feature in your grow plans your plants won't get so tall that they're unmanageable. In fact, for such a sativa heavy strain, Dragon's Teeth doesn't offer a lot in the way of cultivation challenges. The SAGE influence does a lot to calm down the usually more wild sativa side of things, and as the breeders hoped, it also brought a lot of strength and stability to the sativa growth pattern. As well as having stronger stems and branches than most sativas, and growing more of a bush than a Christmas tree, Dragon's Teeth also displays an incredible resistance to pests and especially mites. You also shouldn't find mold becoming a problem with your Dragon's Teeth crop, but it's always good to keep up the ventilation and check your buds regularly. After a 70-day indoor flowering period you'll find yourself ready to bring in a medium-high harvest of medium-dense buds that have filled out towards the end of the growing period. With deep green serrated leaves and hints of white, your buds will look sativa through and through.

Acumen Genetics, USA

Sativa-Dominant

Genetics: Sativa Spirit x SAGE

Potency: THC 18%

acumengenetics.com

The breeders at Acumen have achieved something quite spectacular in creating a plant with such indica-influenced growing patterns but a pure sativa high. The Dragon's Teeth high is an incredibly energetic, motivating one with lots of creativity and mental clarity. This is the kind of strain you need to get shit done, and the delicious taste of blackberries with a hint of gasoline certainly makes you want to partake more often than not. Fantastic work with a great strain!

Early Durban Gold #1

Canada's Limestone City Seeds are an integral part of the Royal Canadian Marijuana Collective, a medical breeder's collective that exists north of the border. For this Early Durban Gold #1, they've crossed the offspring of a Durban Poison and an Early Girl with a Guerilla Gold #5 plant, making a small but powerful plant that yields buds bigger than you would think possible.

Getting its grow structure from its Durban Poison grandparent, Early Durban Gold #1 is a tall, bountiful plant that grows into a Christmas tree shape. This strain is a little too much of everything to be comfortably grown indoors, so this one is unfortunately one for the outdoor growers only. The good news is that she'll truly flourish under the hot sun of the great outdoors, and you should end up with fairly huge plants holding good sized colas that are gorgeously coated in resin. When the harvest time comes in mid-September, you'll find that your yield is actually heavier than it looked; don't forget to roll some finger hash after trimming for a great early treat.

Limestone City Seeds of the Royal Canadian Marijuana Collective, Canada

Sativa-Dominant

Genetics: (Durban Poison x Early Girl) x Guerilla Gold #5

Potency: THC 14%

rcmcollective.ca

A sharp, sweet, and piney flavor, as well as a smell of licorice, give way to a balanced and cerebral high that has just enough of a body buzz to help medical users, as well as recreational users. Durban Poison lovers will adore this strain—if they don't already!

Early Pearl

Holland's Sensi Seeds always seem to create the plants that you didn't even know you wanted, so it's no surprise that Early Pearl is another stellar strain from the stalwarts of the Dutch cannabis scene. Released in the mid-80s, Early Pearl, like Sensi's other Early strains, has been around so long that it sometimes goes to ironic roller disco parties wearing neon headbands and lycra, although if you mention that she will deny it. Although Early Pearl's genetics are a closely guarded secret, she's the pick of the litter at the Sensi offices and she's proven to be fantastic breeding stock for hybrids that need a bit of power and kick in them. In short, she's a badass.

As a 75% sativa, this plant is a tall one that works best when grown outdoors rather than in, as it was bred to be great for shorter summers like those in the north of Europe and especially Holland. The breeders recommend starting your crop indoors in pots at the end of winter then transplanting your crop outdoors when the Spring equinox passes. Go for a space with the most possible light exposure and you should see your transferred plant start to blossom right before your very eyes. Be sure to leave a lot of space for each plant, as these ladies can reach the same height as a small tree (seriously). In the case of below-freezing temperatures, your Early Pearl plants may suffer, so a greenhouse could be a good choice if your area suffers from cold snaps. Early Pearl's colas are so thick and dense you'd think they were modeled on the arms of a professional weightlifter. The good news here is that if any wannabe thieves find your grow just before harvest time, you can actually use the colas as weapons of self defense; buds this hard can knock a dude right out. Even the deep, intense green of the plants is also somewhat intimidating. Despite everything, the flowering period of this strain is only between 50 and 70 days, meaning that plants are generally ready for harvest around the first week of September or even earlier. Get your friends over to help for this, as your yields will be huge and the job will be a tough but worthwhile one!

Sensi Seeds, Holland

Sativa-Dominant

Genetics: Early Pearl from The Seed Bank

sensiseeds.com

The huge, tight buds of Early Pearl explode into a spicy, almost Haze-like flavor and one hell of a thick smoke. The high is just as hectic, and is powerful enough that your enormous yields should last you (and your spouse, your friends, and your entire damn family) a good long while! Early Pearl is a great stash to have on hand at any time, and is always fun to bring out when old stoners come visit you. One puff and they'll remember that time, way back when, that they grew Early Pearl themselves.

East Coast Sour Diesel (clone only)

Illuminati Seeds is the genetics project of Inkognyto, a stellar U.S.-based breeder who seems to be shaking up the apple cart in a really great way at the moment. Seeing far too many West Coast versions of Sour Diesel for his liking, this breeder decided to rep the other side of the country for this fantastic sativa-dominant cross. For this version of the classic, he's taken an Original Diesel and the legendary DNL. If that wasn't impressive enough, consider the fact that, between them, these two strains comprise genetics from Chemdawg, MassSuperSkunk, Sensi Northern Lights, RFK Skunk, Hawaiian Sativa and another big hunk of Northern Lights.

This Sour Diesel was born, along the way, from a Chemdawg offspring known as UnderDawg, Daywrecker, or Diesel #1, depending on who you are talking to. This strain is currently only available in clone form, so the good news is that you won't have to go through the germination process and you'll definitely get a female plant. As soon as your clones get over the transplanting, you'll find that they exhibit vigorous growth right from the start and all the crop will have some good branching. There can be a good amount of stretch in these bad boys if you're not careful, so if you're growing indoors be sure to keep your lights as close to the leaves as you can without burning them or causing any damage. They'll experience a growth spurt just after being flipped into flower, so be sure to flip them early on so they don't get all skeletal and take over your whole grow room. Early in the flowering stage they'll start to smell as dank as you like; super fuel-like with an undercurrent of stinging bitterness that feels like it's burning your nostrils. This strain grows beautifully under a T5, although it will do pretty well no matter what kind of lighting it's exposed to. The colas will start to fill out and get nice and sturdy in the middle of flowering, and the rest of your energy should be spent keeping the smell from becoming a huge issue; dealing with it before your neighbors smell it should be your primary concern!

Illuminati Seeds by Inkognyto, USA

Sativa-Dominant

Genetics: Original Diesel x DNL

Potency: THC 15-17%

As soon as you inhale the smoke of East Coast Sour Diesel you'll see the electric high running towards you from the horizon and then, before you know it, it'll be on you, giving you a crazy intense head rush and a good ol' dose of euphoria. When that calms down a little, the heavy muscle relaxant and pain relief will kick in, making this strain great for medical users as well as recreational tokers.

Easy Ryder

Lowryder by Canada's the Joint Doctor comes up in conversation so regularly with my more straight edge friends that I've memorized the Joint Doctor's website URL and I now just send people there. If you're not a pot grower, the idea that you can get super awesome bud in just 60 days is apparently amazing to you—in fact, I am a pot grower and it's still amazing to me. Regardless, it's hard to overstate the impact that the auto-flowering Lowryder had on the worldwide cannabis community when it was released, and the impact that its offspring continue to have on a market that can't get enough of them.

For this strain, the Doctor took the second version of his most famous creation and crossed it with an Auto AK-47 that is as amazing as it sounds. As a stabilized F1 cross this is a gorgeous little plant that, despite being slightly sativa-dominant, won't get much beyond 2 feet in height and will finish in 56 days of flowering. Yep, you heard me. 56 days. Tell that to your non-pot growing friends and see them shit the bed. The very best traits of the two parent strains have been teased out and caressed lovingly with Easy Ryder, leading them into a harmonious relationship in which they barely even argue about who lost the TV remote. The Auto AK-47 brings a very typically indica style of growing to the table, with a squat stature and lots of side branching, while the carefully selected Lowryder 2 phenotyope brings a phenomenal amount of resin production and a fruity aroma that will tickle your senses and leave them smiling. Easy Ryder grows gorgeously both indoors and out, although it's really made for indoor production if you ask me. The best conditions for growth, as recommended by the breeder, are 20 hours of light and 4 hours of darkness through the entire life cycle of the plant; being an auto, this strain needs a change in light cycle to flip into flower and the more light you can throw at it, the more bud you'll get in the end. Think of it this way: with such a short life of just 70 days from germination to harvest, it needs all the energy it can get! Outdoor growers can manage multiple harvests per season, but the best time is May-August. With a huge yield per harvest, those that can rake in a few cycles before November shows its face will be laughing all the way to the...well, anywhere. You'll just be that high.

A nice berry, fruity taste might come as a bit of a surprise to those expecting a harsher smoke, and the wonderfully balanced high is just what you're hoping for; enough buzz and energy to make this super fun weed made easy.

High Bred Seeds by the Joint Doctor, Canada

Sativa-Dominant

Genetics: Automatic AK-47 x Lowryder #2 F1

Potency: THC 19%

jointdoctordirect.com

PHOTOS BY DAVID STRANGE

Fast Skunk

It must have come as quite a shock to Holland's De Sjamaan Seeds when they turned around one day and realized they'd got a more dedicated following than Justin Bieber, Michael Jackson, and John Lennon put together, but don't have too much sympathy for them; when they decided to keep putting out strains as fantastic as this Fast Skunk, they must have known that they were going to get some serious and enduring love from the worldwide cannabis community! Such great work deserves great praise, and I put myself up there with the most fanatical lovers of De Sjamaan strains. Fast Skunk, as you might have guessed from the name, is a fast-flowering Skunk hybrid created from a Skunk #1 plant and an Early Pearl from Sensi Seeds. Impatient sativa lovers, this plant is for you!

Indoor growers will unfortunately find themselves left out of the Fast Skunk party, as this is a strain that is only suitable for outdoor cultivation. However, outdoor growers can rejoice, as this is one of the easiest and best outdoor strains currently on the mar-

De Sjamaan, Holland

Sativa-Dominant

Genetics: Skunk #1 x Early Pearl

Potency: THC 15%

sjamaan.com

ket. Even if this is your first outdoor grow, you will find Fast Skunk to be more easygoing than a That '70s Show marathon on a lazy Sunday morning, and if you're an experienced sativa cultivator this will be an absolute walk in the park for you. This strain has few needs, but it does need to enjoy a lot of direct sunlight to reach its full potential. Although she can grow up to 10 feet, Fast Skunk can finish growing at a few feet smaller in certain conditions, and if you plant late in the season expect her to stop at about medium height. In that instance, you can easily grow this strain in a balcony space. This variety is particularly resistant to mold and other types of fungus, a trait that will be well appreciated by those in more humid climates. You'll also find that your crop is quite hardy, thanks to a fairly strong structure and nice, thick stems. The most fantastic thing about this strain, however, is right there in the name: it's fast. Ridiculously fast, actually, for such a strong sativa strain. She'll flower in an impressive 63 days, and at harvest, expect to bring in around 500 grams per square yard of grow space; not bad for such a short flowering period!

A warm, sweet taste and a nice smooth smoke will give way to a gorgeously cosy Skunk stone that's mostly in the head and just enough in the body. Potent enough for you to feel it, but not so strong that you can't toke in the daytime for fear of passing out. This is great wake 'n bake pot.

Fruit of the Gods

Given the number of new seed companies that have sprung up and set off running in the last decade or so, Holland's Delta 9 Labs seem almost ancient these days. Yet their outpourings are just as fresh as they always have been, and the wonderful sativa-dominant Fruit of the Gods is a great testament to this fact! Comprising some fantastic genetics from a Northern Lights #5 Haze mother and a Skunk #1 father (and how proud they must be), Fruit of the Gods was always destined to be a real crowd-pleaser. This plant is definitely on the tall side, and you'll need to exercise some patience in the flowering stage as it takes a good 84 days to finish, but believe me when I say it's well worth the wait. If you live in a warmer climate, you're lucky, as this plant produces 25-50% more when grown outdoors in this kind of environment. Experienced indoor growers might want to go hydroponic to try to match these yields. Even with plants kept to a maximum height of 4 feet, you can expect to rake in at least 50 grams per plant. Not bad!

Delta 9 Labs, Holland

Sativa-Dominant

Genetics: Northern Lights #5 Haze x Skunk #1

Potency: THC 17%

delta9labs.com

When the fruity smoke clears and the Hazey taste is lingering on your tongue, expect the clear and uplifting high to overtake you within a few minutes. Before you know it, you'll be jumping out of your seat to clean the fridge out with a grin plastered to your face.

Golden Goat

The Golden Goat was the name of a particularly disastrous Chinese / Jamaican crossover restaurant near where I grew up, so the smells of Jerk Kung Pow and Sweet and Sour Goat will forever sting my nostrils when I think of this strain. Thankfully, the beautiful aroma of this IrieGenetics Colorado plant helps to brush away those memories on a sea of Island Sweet Skunk, Hawaiian and Romulan genetics.

Originally created in Kansas, this strain came about when a cheeky male Hawaiian / Romulan cross managed to pollinate Mr. Dank's freak Island Sweet Skunk. IrieGenetics got hold of a cut of the resulting strain and backcrossed it into stabilization. Growers can expect a solid structure with lots of branching, although plants can exhibit a lot of trim when flowering. Keep your eye on these ladies as they can tend to shoot up when your back is turned; don't be afraid to resort to some LST if necessary for your grow space. This plant prefers indoor growing and will be finished in 60 days with a heavy harvest, so be prepared!

The rule with Golden Goat is that you can always smoke more, but you can't smoke less. Golden Goat is a hard hitter, so smoke carefully and ease yourself into the energetic, mood enhancing high and your experience will be just lovely.

IrieGenetics Colorado, USA

Sativa-Dominant

Genetics: Island Sweet Skunk x (Hawaiian x Romulan)

Potency: THC 24%

iriegeneticscolorado.com

Goldstar

Bodhi Seeds is a great company based out of the U.S., although their love of good genetics obviously spreads far beyond the borders of the homeland, as the parentage of this fantastic plant goes to show. A blend of the mostly-indica Sensi Star and a Malawi Gold plant that's mostly sativa, this plant is a balanced one that's as gorgeous as it is impressive.

Goldstar is from the Gold Star Genetics collection from Bodhi Seeds, and was created when the breeder decided to let his oldschool sweet turpentine phenotype of Sensi Star get a little down and dirty with a sturdy Malawi Gold male. The successful little babies were then backcrossed over time to stabilize the line. As it stands, Goldstar is now able to be grown both indoors and outdoors, although the breeder suggests that to get the very best out of the strain you should grow it out in the great wide open. If you do choose to grow indoors, however, you'll find this to be a very manageable strain that takes well to training and exhibits some super vigorous growth.

Bodhi Seeds, USA

Sativa-Dominant

Genetics: Sensi Star x Malawi Gold

Potency: THC 18-24%

breedbay.co.uk

cannabis-seeds-bank.co.uk

As these plants were all created in a totally organic environment, it's recommended that they be cultivated in the same sort of set up. Despite the heavy sativa influence, this plant has almost no stretch, which is good news for greenhouse growers, and a warm environment will bring out a rich terpene signature. The vigor of this plant is maintained throughout the flowering stage as well as the vegetative stage, so be sure to keep a good eye on your stems and buds if you're growing in high humidity, as bud rot and mold can take hold without you even noticing. No one likes to lose half their stash or half their crop to the white-powdered devil. Depending on whether you're growing indoors or outdoors, your flowering time will be somewhere between 10 weeks and 14 weeks, but be sure to let your plants go until they look good and ready. Your yield will be nothing short of incredible; these plants kick out buds as if it's easy.

After a good drying process (thick buds take longer to dry; ensure that yours are good and dried out before you cure them) you'll be astounded by how gorgeous these buds are. This huge bag appeal is great news for anyone growing for commercial purposes, but a bigger draw is the beautiful mint and pine smell that you'll get from your buds. Bust them open and pack a bowl before you get too entranced and you'll experience the trippy head high that the Malawi Gold brings to the table.

Grand Daddy Blue Dream

Any time you wave a Grand Daddy Purp strain in my face I'm definitely going to sit up and take notice, and so, I think, will any lovers of Blue strains when they lay eyes on the absolutely gorgeous buds of this Granddaddy Purp Genetics strain. Grand Daddy Blue Dream is a potent and majestic sativa-dominant hybrid from the purveyors of Grand Daddy Purp, although the exact genetics of this Blue Dream are kept as a closely guarded secret. After all, if you had the recipe for the world's greatest burger, wouldn't you keep it close to your chest?

This plant is a tall one, but it won't reach the epic 14 feet that some sativas like to get to. Indoor growers will be thrilled to hear that they, too, can enjoy cultivating this plant, although if you're a medical user with a small closet grow you might find that this strain is going to be a drain on your limited space; greenhouse grows or outdoor patches are the very best options for this kind of strain. As with all medical strains, it's recommended that Grand Daddy Blue Dream be grown in a fully organic set up, preferably in soil, but this strain is one that can adapt well to different environments. However, soil will always be its favorite home. We all know that I'm a huge admirer of buds that like to foxtail, and this trait of Grand Daddy Blue Dream is one of my favorites; to watch it grow is to watch a work of art being painted. Its sharp, serrated leaves flourish into a deep green, which is offset by the pure white crystals that emerge from them. Eventually these crystals will take on a blue hue, contributing to the colorful palate of greens, oranges, blues, and whites of the plant when it reaches full maturity. Though the flowering stage isn't exactly short, sitting around 10 weeks depending on your grow techniques, the finished buds are certainly worth the wait. Your yield will certainly be on the heavy side, and you'll be so dazzled by the sapphire buds that the harvesting process will fly by and you'll barely notice that you were sat trimming those beauties for days on end.

Granddaddy Purp Genetics, USA

Sativa-Dominant

granddaddypurp.com

Granddaddy Purp Genetics creates strains for medical use, so patients will find that this is a true Blue Dream for them. The buds smell Skunky, but when you get to taste the thick smoke the sourness of the flavor will hit you smack between the eyes. The effect is a relaxing one, great for muscular pain and spasms, and those with chronic stomach pain and anxiety will find this to be a strain that's perfect for them. This is an ideal strain for use prior to bed time, and can help those suffering from pain to get some much-needed rest.

Harlequin

I like to think that the guys and girls at Green Haven Genetics have named this plant Harlequin because they're big comic book fans, just like me. Beyond its awesome name, though, this strain has a hell of a lot to offer, as even a brief glance over its parentage will show. Comprising Thai, Swiss, and Nepalese genetics mixed with a Colombian Gold from the 70s, this sativa-dominant hybrid has some serious credentials. Its leaves have been tested at 2% THC and 4% CBD, making it a high-CBD strain in a big way. Currently available in clone form only, Bay Area residents are most likely to find themselves the lucky owners of this strain for the time being.

For a sativa, this is an incredibly hardy plant that clearly enjoys the influence that the indica genetics have over the strength of its structure. Although taller than an indica, this plant can easily be kept to a height that's manageable. If you prefer, however, to see your sativas reach for the sky and reach their full potential height, you won't be disappointed here. With a short vegetative period she'll soon be ready to be flipped into flower, and will surprise you by starting to bloom a lot quicker than you might expect. The breeders at Green Haven recall seeing flowers as long as your finger just 2 weeks after the flip, which is the sort of thing that makes any true grower ridiculously excited. Towards the end of the flowering stage, the buds will be absolutely caked in resin, to the point where you can barely tell there are any buds there and it looks like someone just threw a bag of sugar at a tree. Of course, this is always good news for the wannabe hash maker. As the sugary crystals start to really show themselves, the weight of the flowers will start to be too much for the branches to hold, meaning that you'll need to give the plant some additional support to hold its blossoming load. Staking your plants will be perfect, but be sure to do it sooner rather than later. Give her a full 70 days to finish, and then she'll most likely require a full three weeks to properly dry, given the weight of the buds and the amount of resin therein. While you're waiting, you'll be able to enjoy the fingerhash made from after the manicure; and trust me, there'll be enough!

Bred specifically to produce some high-grade hash and oils for medical patients, Harlequin is a fairly rare strain that is important to the medical cannabis movement. Ready yourself for some of the best hash you've ever tasted, because boy, this plant really delivers!

Green Haven Genetics, USA

Sativa-Dominant

Genetics: Colombian Gold (1970s version) x Thailand x Switzerland x Nepalese

Potency: THC 2% / CBD 4%

greenhavengenetics.com

Hawaiian Wave

As something of a surfer back in my glory days (and by glory days I mean a few years ago when I could get in the ocean without needing a lie down), I would have jumped on this strain hard and fast, refusing to smoke anything else and declaring it to be "radical" to anyone who had the patience to listen. Now that I'm a little older, less fit, and not even regretful about selling my board for new iPod speakers, I can appreciate this Ripper Seeds strain in a real way. Spain's Ripper Seeds took a gorgeous landrace plant from Hawaii and chose it to be their breeding stock for Hawaiian Wave, thinking long and hard about what might be the perfect parent to complement the landrace's wild nature. They finally decided on their own Double Glock strain, a sweet but powerful plant that knocks most tokers onto their knees.

As Double Glock is a 100% indica strain from the remote valleys of Afghanistan, these genetics serve to counterbalance the 100% sativa of the Hawaiian landrace, meaning that your Hawaiian Wave plants won't be 14 feet tall with a flowering time longer than your puberty. In fact, this strain has been tamed so much that it can be grown both indoors and out, although outdoor growers might just have the edge in getting higher yields and a more interesting experience of growing this variety. Still, it can get a little taller than you want it to even indoors, so the breeders recommend only allowing for a 1 or 2 week vegetative period before forcing your babies into flowering. The plants will at least double and maybe even triple in height after the flip, so remember to stake them early on to avoid any issues later on in flowering. This strain should be fairly resistant to mold and will do fine in climates with a lot of humidity, but might struggle slightly when exposed to excessive bouts of cold. The flowering period will be fairly long although not overly so; generally about 10 or 11 weeks for most areas and about 80 days indoors. Expect a high yield, especially outdoors, with huge colas of pale colors and gorgeous greens! This plant is a Hawaiian through and through.

Ripper Seeds, Spain

Sativa-Dominant

Genetics: Hawaiian Landrace x Double Glock

Potency: THC 14%

ripperseeds.com

I'm a huge fan of strains from the 50th state, and not just because they make those delicious biscuits there that seem to be tailor-made for a stoner with the munchies. No, it's the good looking buds, the fruity, crisp-ocean-air taste of the smoke and, most of all, the flying, euphoric high that makes me a fan of Hawaiian weed—and Hawaiian Wave gives me all this and so much more.

Haze Plum Purple Passion

America's Stoney Girl Gardens grow their plants strong, and they grow them well. This unreleased strain originally came from a friend of the Stoney Girl Gardens breeder whose brother-in-law, the original breeder, was tragically killed in a glider accident. Preserving these fantastic genetics over the years has become a labor of love, and the photogenic nature of the plant makes it easy to remember a lost life in a positive light.

Growing to no more than 4 feet in height, Haze Plum Purple Passion is a relatively tame strain that's easy to grow and will make your garden look perfectly picturesque. It enjoys temperatures of around 70 to 80 and has a good resistance to pests and mold. Outdoor growers will see this plant truly flourish; the absolutely stunning looking buds will grow in shades of orange, yellow, and peach, and your harvest will be more than sizable.

Stoney Girl Gardens, USA

Sativa-Dominant

Potency: THC 17%

gro4me.com

Great for appetite stimulation as well as treating PTSD, Haze Plum Purple Passion is a great strain for all different types of medical marijuana users, especially those dealing with depression and eating disorders. Recreational users will experience extreme munchies and big grins all around.

Holy Purple Thai

I dread to think the amount of airmiles that the breeder at SnowHigh Seeds has racked up over the years, as his breeding stock encompasses most of the countries in the world. Holy Purple Thai is a combination of Big Sur Holy Weed from Bodhi Seeds and a Purple Thai landrace sativa hybrid that grows pink and gives a killer sativa high.

A real pleasure to grow, Holy Purple Thai can express several different pheno-types, none of which demand that much talent or attention from their grower. This is great news for newbie sativa growers who are looking for a simple but impressive strain to hone their skills with. With a good amount of stretch, this plant can end up tall, but it won't produce loose buds; instead, they're fairly dense and absolutely drip-ping in resin. Depending which pheno you're growing, your flowering time will be somewhere between 9 and 11 weeks, and your crop will be as pink as a new born girl's wardrobe before you bring it down for the chop.

Sticky, sweet, and gorgeous to smoke, Holy Purple Thai buds look good enough to lick—although I wouldn't recommend that. The high is very strong, very clear, and very euphoric, meaning that you might just find yourself running naked through the streets wearing nothing but a smile. I can't think of a better way to spend a day.

PHOTOS BY SNOW

SnowHigh Seeds, USA

Heirloom Sativa Hybrid

Genetics: Bodhi's Big Sur Holy Weed x Purple Thai

Jack 47

Spain's Sweet Seeds definitely know a modern cannabis classic when they see one—or, in the case of this strain, two. Jack 47 is a fantastic mash up of two strains that send tokers insane in the membrane: Jack Herer and the much-lauded AK-47. The Sweet Seeds breeders took their "stud" plant, a male AK-47 that had proved itself time and time again to be an amazing father plant, producing progeny that give huge yields as well as a strong high, and crossed this with a female Jack Herer (Jackie Herer?) that had been used to great effect in their popular Black Jack strain. The result is a strain that's very worthy of attention; a super yielder with a massive high that's a fantastic choice for hash making.

As a 75% sativa, Jack 47 grows fairly tall, but it is still short enough to be grown in an indoor environment if that's your jam. However, such a strong sativa influence is bound to cause a little wildness in a plant, and so this strain is not recommended for new growers, or even those who are new to sativa cultivation. Instead, growers with a lot of experience will be able to draw the very best out of this plant and will enjoy the challenges that it offers. Jack 47 grows with great vigor and speed, and it can grow well in almost any environment or system. Low Stress Training can be a great tool to ensure that you get the best out of this plant whatever your grow set up is like. Growers will love the ease with which this strain gives itself over to cloning; the vigor means that the potential sites for cuttings are numerous, and the clones themselves will take root in 7 days when conditions are good. Despite the speed of Jack 47 and the density of its buds, this plant exhibits an extraordinary resistance to mold and bud rot. The flowers of Jack 47 are particularly gorgeous, seemingly growing into themselves and every which way, giving the impression of layers of velvet forming one giant bud. Indoor growers will be taking these gorgeous buds down after about 9.5 weeks of flowering, whereas outdoor growers will need to wait until the end of October. The yield of this plant is nothing short of phenomenal, especially outdoors. You'll have so much bud you'll barely know what to do with it. I expect, obviously, that you'll just smoke it all.

Tokers will recognize the Jack Herer taste and smell in this strain, but once the high sets in they may not be able to recognize their own faces in the mirror. An absolute annihilator of a strain, Jack 47 puts you on another planet entirely. Seriously good bud.

Sweet Seeds, Spain

Sativa-Dominant

Genetics: Jack Herer x AK-47

Potency: THC 18-24% / CBD 1.6%

sweetseeds.es

Jack Diesel

Positronics Seeds from Spain has some serious credentials. Not only are they much appreciated throughout their native Europe and beyond, but the man behind the seed company, the famous Wernard Bruining, started the first ever grow shop in the Netherlands. It was, of course, named Positronics, and this place provided everything that a cannabis grower could ever need. When the grow shop hit hard times, the seed company was taken over by several employees and friends, and the Positronics name and ethos was able to keep going, growing from strength to strength. Today, Positronics can be relied upon to work with only the best genetics, and for this Jack Diesel strain they've used two extremely popular sativa-dominant hybrids: Jack Herer and New York City Diesel. By now, you all know how much of a Diesel fan I am, so to say that this is my kind of strain is something of an understatement.

Jack Diesel is a fantastic example of a strain that's truly greater than the sum of its parts. Despite being borne of spectacular parents, this plant really does hold its own in almost every regard. With a strong, hardy structure and vigorous growth from the vegetative period right through the flowering stage, Jack Diesel looks like it's aiming for the stars even when it's a mere seedling. Medium tall and with lots of energetic growth, this plant can get a little out of hand if you leave it too long indoors, so those growing in restricted space are advised to cut the vegetative stage as short as logically possible. With excessive side branching, this strain can grow spindly if it's given too much space. Almost all plants will need to be staked in the vegetative stage to provide support later on in the flowering period.

Positronics Seeds, Spain

Sativa-Dominant

Genetics: Jack Herer x New York City Diesel

Potency: THC 22% / CBD 0.1%

positronics.eu

It's very important to keep a keen eye on the pH level of this crop; if it gets above 7, you'll notice a yellowing between the veins of the leaves. This can be rectified by adjusting to the correct pH, but prevention is always better than cure so watch out for the pH of your soil and the water you put into it. This strain will enjoy extra zinc, iron, and manganese, and towards the end of the 70 day flowering period your buds will be coming in thick and strong. An average indoor yield is around 500 grams per square yard of grow space, while outdoor cultivators can bring in around 600 grams per plant.

With a taste of tangerines and fuel, this is a flavor you might have to learn to love, but you'll be enamored with the psychoactive, clear, long lasting high from the moment it touches your brain and sends you right into the sky.

Jack the Ripper

So named because it's absolutely killer weed, this strain from the inimitable Subcool and his Team Green Avengers will get you seriously ripped (ah, ha ha...groan). Jack the Ripper is a combination of a P1 of Jack's Cleaner and Space Queen. The Jack's Cleaner parent came from a crossing of Jack Herer and The Cleaner, a strain from breeder Skoosh that contained both Northern Lights #5 and Purple Haze. Named for its smell, which was just like the odor of a cleaning product called Mr. Clean, this strain proved too good to ignore, and eventually it was allowed to pollinate a Jack Herer female, resulting in Jack's Cleaner. This strain has been used in a few hybrids, like Jack's Cleaner Blueberry, but it has never held its own quite like it does in Jack the Ripper. With Romulan, Lamb's Bread, Pluton, and Cindy99 BCGA in its family tree, this strain is almost a thing of legend—just like its namesake.

This strain expresses two main phenotypes, both of which smell like Lemon Haze. One tends to have scents of pine, which is generally how you can tell the difference, al-

Subcool and Team Green Avengers, USA

Sativa-Dominant

Genetics: Jack's Cleaner P1 x Space Queen

Potency: THC 26.6%

tgagenetics.com

though one is considerably shorter than the other, too. The height of this strain varies by the different phenotypes, but none will get excessively tall unless you let them truly flourish in an outdoor environment. The best way to grow this strain is untopped, and it should be allowed a good long vegetative period so that it can grow into its full bushy self. An organic soil grow will be best with Jack the Ripper and it won't need much in the way of nutrients, but if you prefer a hydro grow then you won't find it much trouble either way. Once you flip your Jack crop into flowering you'll be able to see the production ramping up from about day 12, when the spear-shaped white buds begin to show themselves. Indoors or out, you should expect harvest to come around week 8 of flowering, although some phenotypes will run a little longer. Your yield will be moderate to heavy, and you won't need to spend days and days trimming the finished buds.

Your Jack the Ripper nugs will smell like tropical fruits with an undertone of burning hash, and some phenotypes will have a piney scent as well. Like its namesake, this strain will catch you totally unawares and then send you straight towards the light— the only difference being that your light is the blinding shock of an amazing head high rather than the beams of a lantern being held by your Maker. This strain is definitely from heaven rather than From Hell. Plus, it contains THCV which is a possible cure for Parkinson's disease. Not bad, eh?

Jamaican Dream

Spain's Eva Female Seeds are the nicest cannabis breeders you could ever hope to meet. As well as being "muy amable," they're also damn good at what they do, and they seem to improve with every new strain. Jamaican Dream is a strain bred from a Jamaican heirloom, and as a 90% sativa plant it's sure to impress tokers from all walks of life.

Perfect for both indoor and outdoor cultivation, this is a hardy plant that grows in a Christmas tree style and is easy enough to grow that even newbie cultivators will be able to get the best out of it. Outdoors, Jamaican Dream can grow to around 6 feet or more, whereas indoor growers should force flowering at around 2 feet for a final height of 3 feet. The breeders recommend growing under sodium lights and going either medium or heavy with the nutrients to maximize yield. Indoor growers will harvest around 70 grams per plant, while outdoor growers will be able to get at the very least 500 grams from each Jamaican Dream. Flowering time is 42 days, which is incredibly quick, and this translates to a harvest time of the end of September outdoors.

Eva Female Seeds, Spain

Sativa-Dominant

Genetics: Heirloom Jamaican

Potency: THC 17-19%

evaseeds.com

Despite its indica growth style, this strain gives a gorgeous sativa high along with a smell of fresh limes and a taste of burnt wood. A perfect strain for sativa lovers who prefer an indica growing style!

Jamaican Lions

The USA's Natural Ganjahnetics are based in the USA, and apparently have some sort of special portal to a world full of amazing genetics and landrace strains, because damn this is a badass hybrid! As a small collection of breeders and growers that cater to medical marijuana patients, high quality and high CBD levels are of great importance to these guys and they're very much dedicated to their cause. For this great medical strain, they've combined a Mountain Lion strain with a Landrace Jamaican "Yarders" strain to create a hybrid that's 94% sativa and only 6% indica. Growers, hold on to your hats!

As an almost 100% sativa strain with landrace genetics, Jamaican Lions is a plant that's best grown by cultivators who've had at least a little experience growing pure sativa strains in the past. Those who've grown landrace strains before will be able to draw the very best of the best out of this crop, but it might be a little too challenging for new growers or those who've never grown a sativa before. Jamaican Lions can grow to anywhere between 4 and 18 feet tall, which gives you some indication of just what we're dealing with here! Whilst it is possible to grow this strain indoors, it will take no small amount of Low Stress Training and tying down to tame its growth, and even SOG or ScrOG set ups might find it too much to handle. Instead, if possible, grow this strain outdoors and see it blossom into a magnificent plant of monstrous proportions. Looming over the rest of your plants like some sort of demonic giant spider, this plant will do well in West Coast US environments as it was developed right here in the States. It should have a pretty high resistance to pests and also to mold, but it's always good to use high-quality soil and organic nutes where possible. Stake your plants; when they're taller than you and trying to hold onto their loose, sizable buds they're most certainly going to need a little help. After a 10-week flowering period you will bring in a huge yield, but of course those with the biggest plants will have the biggest harvest.

Natural Ganjahnetics, USA

Sativa-Dominant

Genetics: Mountain Lion x Jamaican Yarders (Landrace)

Potency: THC 6.8% / CBD 9.7%

facebook.com/
  natural.ganjahnetics

projectcbd.org

With hints of red and orange highlighting the bright green of the buds, these are some pretty ass nugs and you'll definitely want to show them off. Landrace fans will especially love to see your stash. The high is a very clear, very alert mental high with a body relaxation that belies the heavy sativa genetics of the plant; medical users will find this great as pain relief and an anti-inflammatory thanks to the high CBD content.

Jesus Christ

The name of this strain will annoy the anti-toking Christian pearl clutcher (my mother) as much as it tickles the hippy smoking fan (me). Jesus Christ was born accidentally but became a fantastic example of its type—just like someone I read about once. Can't remember His name though. Anyways, when JC sprouted it very quickly became 100% taller than the rest of the six seeds which were started at the same time. The gardener saw it and said "Jesus Christ that plant is huge!" and a strain was born.

Created by pure chance when a Ghost OG got too close to a soaring Sour Diesel, Jesus Christ showed itself to be impressive enough to hang on to; a prime example of a fantastic sativa-dominant hybrid that can be grown both indoors and out. JC is not too fussy and not too long in flowering, and it may seem that this strain is a little middle of the road at first, but that just makes it an easy grow for those inexperienced in the ways of sativa; you might say that it's a miracle. To preserve that tangy, fuel-like Sour Diesel smell from the parent plant it's best to grow this in an organic soil mix and go easy on the synthetic nutes; remember that quality is the goal with this strain rather than quantity.

Expect a beautifully balanced high with a lot of energy; smoke enough and you might even start believing that you're the son of God.

Green Dream Health Services, USA

Sativa-Dominant

Genetics: Ghost OG x Sour Diesel

greendreamhealth.com

PHOTOS BY RY PRICHARD/KINDREVIEWS.COM

Killer Skunk

I'm not sure what it is about sativa strains in particular that causes people to name them after murderers or serial killers, but this Skunk strain from the UK's Underground Originals is certainly some killer pot. KillerSkunk is a combination of some fantastic genetics, listing Blues and SmellyBerry as its parent strains. Given that UGORG work only with original heirloom and landrace breeding stock, it should come as no surprise that this strain is nothing short of an "extreme hybrid," the likes of which UGORG pride themselves on creating.

SmellyBerry is a Blues and Original Blueberry cross, meaning that although it's a hybrid strain it's got a whole heap of indica in there that manages its growing style and gives the final smoke a body stone effect with a head high cutting through. This indica influence is more than apparent in the KillerSkunk offspring, as this plant won't grow excessively tall but will yield heavily, especially under intense lights. Grown indoors or out, this is a relatively easy plant to cultivate, even if you don't have a whole lot of experience in growing sativa-dominant strains. If your indoor grow space is particularly small, you might consider keeping the vegetative stage quite short and applying Low Stress Training to make the most of the space that you have. This plant is a hardy one and will react well to gentle training, as well as exhibiting some great side branching and a fairly bushy final stature. Don't be afraid to completely pack your grow room with lights, as the more wattage you can get to grow your KillerSkunk plants, the more massive your final yield will be. Charcoal filters are going to be absolutely necessary for those growing indoors. The smell of this strain close to harvest time is stifling at best, and will alert everyone in your town to your grow op at worst. After forcing flowering, you should be seeing your plants reach full maturity between 7 and 9 weeks depending on your climate or your grow environment. Be sure not to pull the plants down too early and you should bring in about a gram per watt of light indoors.

Underground Originals, UK

Sativa-Dominant

Genetics: Blues x SmellyBerry

Potency: THC 16%

ugorg.com

The heavy smell that sets in near harvest will take hold of your KillerSkunk buds and refuse to let go, meaning that after a short curing period these babies are going to stink to high heaven. Aromas of hash, lemon, and pine will seduce your nostrils, and the dark green buds will look good enough to eat. Spark up a J to experience the incredibly happy, social high that has no paranoia side effects. Medical users may find this strain useful for managing spasms and muscular tension.

King Congo

Spain's Tropical Seeds company aren't afraid to tackle the difficult pure sativa strains; in fact, they revel in the challenge. This pure variety is a combination of Ciskei P3 and Congo Point Noire genetics, and though that list may read as gobbledegook for some tokers, connoisseurs will know that this strain has great genes and is always going to be something special.

It's not easy to get a pure sativa strain that's suitable for indoor growth, but King Congo is one of those rare strains that's happy in a grow room despite its genetic heritage. It's a medium sized plant that yields average to heavy indoors, but outdoors it can really come into its own and will provide a lot more bud than you might expect. A very attractive plant, exhibiting deep green buds littered with snow white hairs, King Congo grows fists of flowers that are almost as exciting to grow as they are to harvest. The flowering period sits somewhere between 65 and 75 days, and these buds should be dried and cured well for bests results.

Tropical Seeds Company, Spain

Pure F1 Sativa

Genetics: Congo Pointe Noire x Ciskei P4 F1 (South African Highland Sativa)

Potency: THC 18%

tropicalseedscompany.com

King Congo has a smoke that smells of lemon and lime, with a sweet undertone and an earthy aftertaste. A very fun, creative, and active high, this is a perfect wake 'n bake strain that will make your workday go with a bang and keep you up all night, too.

La Roja

The always confusing Jamaica Seeds, who are actually based out of Spain, have combined two Latin American classics into one strain with La Roja, a sativa-dominant beauty. The iconic Panama Red, the favorite strain of the 70s, meets a Colombian sativa that's as gorgeous as it is powerful, and as ever, we get to reap the benefits. Hooray! ¡Ándale!

Outdoors, this strain can climb to an absolutely high 14 feet in height, so indoor growers might struggle to keep her tame enough for their space. The payoff from this difficult-to-deal-with structure, however, is that your La Roja plant will produce the kind of volume that makes other growers truly jealous. After a nice 12 weeks of flowering, your plants will be straining under the weight of their buds and begging to be harvested. True to her name, La Roja will exhibit reddish-purple hues towards the end of flowering, especially when subjected to some colder temperatures.

When the breeders describe this high as "soaring," they aren't lying. There can't be much indica influence in this strain as there seems to be nothing to constrain the energetic, crazy happy sativa effect. La Roja will plant wings on your back and send you flying whether you like it or not. And trust me, you will like it. A fantastic strain that harks back to the glory days of sativas, La Roja is a welcome addition to any garden.

Jamaica Seeds, Spain

Sativa-Dominant

Genetics: Panama Red x Colombian

Potency: THC 20%

jamaicaseeds.com

Lemon Alien

I'm a huge fan of the Ridley Scott movie series starring Sigourney Weaver as Ripley, and I can't help but wish that somewhere along the line they'd managed to slip Lemon Alien in as a movie title, maybe instead of Alien 3 or even Alien vs. Predator. I'd much rather see some horrific Alien-citrus fruit combination than watch either of those two movies again. In reality, Lemon Alien isn't a moderately entertaining celluloid take on Ripley's adventures with marmalade, it's a sativa-dominant cannabis strain from La Plata Labs, a young seed company based out of the U.S. For this strain, they've brought together not Captain Dallas and Executive Officer Kane but a Super Lemon Haze from GHS and Alien Bubba—which still sounds like it would make a better sequel than Alien: Resurrection.

This strain is almost 50/50 with a slight bias towards sativa, so it will be a great choice for indoor growers, for whom the breeder decided to create this plant. The breeders originally introduced Alien Bubba to their favorite cut of GHS's Super Lemon Haze in order to add potency, structure, and faster flowering, and they've certainly succeeded in those goals. Not only is this plant incredibly easy to grow, it also branches out to grow magnificent spear-shaped colas that, by the time harvest rolls around, will be sticky with resin and desperate to be plucked. There are no particular prickly pests that like to ravage Lemon Alien (would you be stupid enough to take on a creature with a worryingly phallic tongue?) but the vigorous growth of this strain means that cultivators should keep a sharp eye out for any white growth or other telltale signs of mold and bud rot, especially in the later stages of the flowering period. This strain will be fully finished and mature in between 8 and 9 weeks, which is super fast for a strain that leans towards the sativa side of things. Unlike a true Xenomorph, Lemon Alien is a colorful little beast, with its red and yellow leaves seemingly monochrome next to its buds, which could well have been rolled around on a freshly-painted Jackson Pollock before being placed on your Lemon Alien crops.

La Plata Labs, USA

Sativa-Dominant

Genetics: GHS's Super Lemon Haze x Alien Bubba

Potency: THC 16%

laplatalabs.com

After harvest, you should be able to roll yourself some pretty damn good finger hash thanks to the thick layer of resin on the outside of these buds. A good curing period is also recommended because curing brings out the amazing taste of this strain. The sharp, sweet lemon candy flavor is a gorgeous accent to the energetic and sophisticated high that eventually melts into a mild body buzz. Just heavenly.

Lemonator

Canada's Next Generation Seed Company began in 1997 and aims to be a reliable source of good quality genetics and some truly interesting hybrid plants. With over a decade in the business, these guys have a great reputation in their native Great White North and their message continues to spread to the U.S. and Europe with every new strain that they bring out. Lemonator, as you may guess from the name, is one for the fans of citrusy strains, but a little less obvious is the fact that it's a great Haze strain, as the offspring of a Llimonet Haze that's been crossed with an indica. This wonderful hybrid tastes like homemade lemonade on a sunny day and has a balanced high that hits all the right buttons.

The Lemonator family is a truly international one, as the sativa parent hails originally from Spain while the indica parent came from "oot west," or British Columbia to us Non-Canadians. Although any international relationship can be tricky, these two crazy kids in love made it work, and as such, Lemonator holds both a Canadian and an E.U. passport. Suitable for both indoor and outdoor growing environments, but best suited to a European or Canadian climate that doesn't get too hot in the summer, Lemonator is a great choice for both commercial and personal grows as it is an above average yielder with a unique high and taste. This will be a tall plant that takes well to meshing techniques indoors, so if you've been looking for a strain to try with a ScrOG set up, Lemonator might be the one you've been waiting for. If you're trying to reduce the size as much as possible, hanging weights on the branches can be surprisingly effective. Outdoors, this strain will soar into the sky. Lemonator is resistant to many pests and problems but it is especially great in warding off botrytis and other funghi. As with many of my favorite sativas, Lemonator plants foxtail beautifully in the flowering stage; as they mature, they become even more beautiful and interesting. These plants will be fully mature in 10 weeks from forced flowering, which equates to a harvest at the very beginning of October for outdoor growers. Your yield will be sizable but not so immense that you put your back out whilst hauling your buds down.

Next Generation Seed Company, Canada

Sativa-Dominant

Genetics: Llimonet Haze x Unknown Indica

Potency: THC 15%

greenlifeseeds.com

The smoke of Lemonator is thick and citrusy, with sweet overtones and a cheeky hint of spicy Haze taste underneath everything. The high is pure Haze: euphoric, creative, and the perfect thing to put a spring in your step in the morning. Take advantage of your sticky buds and make some great quality hash; you won't regret it!

Mango Haze

Named after the state I find myself in when mango season rolls around and I buy a whole box of them in the midst of a munchies attack, this strain from Holland's Mr. Nice Seedbank has the sort of family tree that makes even Frances Bean Cobain jealous. With a quadruple dose of Haze as well as some Skunk #1 and Northern Lights #5 in the mix, Mango Haze has it all.

At just over 50% sativa, this is a great strain for indoor growing, and if you're short on grow space the breeder recommends going straight to forced flowering with a rooted clone or seed. Your finished plant will top out at about 4 or 5 feet, whilst outdoors it can get much bigger. Prune your lower branches to encourage greater yields, and don't worry about mold; it won't pose a threat to your crop. Whether you're growing organic or in hydro this strain should be a breeze, and after 66 days of flowering you should see something in the region of 500 grams per square yard of grow room. Experienced growers will be able to get much more from their harvest, depending on how they organize their lights and the nutrient program they use.

Fruity, delicious, and very, very resinous, Mango Haze buds explode into a riot of cerebral rushes and gorgeous vibes with exceptional mango aromas.

Mr. Nice Seedbank, Holland

Sativa-Dominant

Genetics: Northern Lights #5/Haze x Skunk/Haze

Potency: THC 19%

mrnice.nl

Micky Kush

We've come to expect nothing less than the best from Subcool and Team Green Avengers, and they wouldn't dream of providing anything that wasn't top quality. Micky Kush is a cross between the fantastic Jack the Ripper and a Sweet Irish Kush that finishes quickly and makes for a great daytime smoke!

This plant expresses three main phenotypes; an Irish Kush dominant, a Jack dominant, and one that's a mix of the two. All grow to a medium height with a good amount of stretch, so the breeders recommend topping out the plants and rounding them out into a bush shape. A soil grow is perfect for this strain, and it won't require much in the way of additional feeding or special treatment; it's surprisingly hardy. After 56 days you'll be pulling down a medium to heavy yield, but don't forget to stop and admire the gorgeous, deep green, fatty colas and let your jaw drop in awe.

This is a one-hitter-quitter for rookie smokers, and even those with more than a little toking time under their belts might be left bewildered by this heavy high. Sour Kushy tones play with scents of lemon, and as the smoke clears you'll be gliding high, starting your day off with a bang. ADHD sufferers and those with depression may find that all three phenos of this strain are of great benefit to them and can help many of us to get through our day.

PHOTOS BY MATT DYLAN

Subcool and Team Green Avengers, USA
Sativa-Dominant
Genetics: Sweet Irish Kush x Jack The Ripper
Potency: THC 28.6% / CBD 0.6%
tgagenetics.com

Neo Blizzard

Spain's Evil Seeds have really pulled something special out of the bag with this strain. I'm not quite sure where the name comes from (fans of the Matrix and that weird ice cream thing you get at fast food places? A winning word in Scrabble? Maybe they pulled the name out of a hat?) but when a strain is purported to be that strong, you really have to sit up and take notice. For this strain, the breeders at Evil Seeds have taken the already epic Matanuska Tundra and bred it with a Congolese sativa plant that brings in even more fantastic sativa genetics. The resulting plant is three quarters sativa, one quarter indica, giving the final smoke that bit of extra punch and making the plant a little easier to grow.

In terms of cultivation, the little indica influence in NeoBlizzard serves to take the edge off what would otherwise be a seriously severe sativa variety. As it stands, NeoBlizzard won't grow as tall as pure sativa plants will, but might still post a problem for indoor growers unless they take steps to keep it nice and tamed whilst still in the vegetative state. The indica genetics add some bushiness to the sativa growing style, and your finished buds will be incredibly easy to manicure thanks to the great calyx-to-leaf ratio. Indoor flowering will run to around 70 or 80 days, which is pretty fast for this type of plant. This translates to a mid-October harvest date for those of you growing outdoors. Although the manicuring of these buds will be easy, the harvesting won't, as the huge, huge production of these plants will make cutting the buds down the job of a few people at least. Crack some dark ales, invite your friends over, and don't forget to roll yourselves some finger hash when you're done.

Evil Seeds, Spain

Sativa-Dominant

Genetics: Matanuska Tundra x Congolese

Potency: THC 20-22%

evilseeds.es

When they say that NeoBlizzard is a force to be reckoned with, they aren't messing around. There's something about this strain that just screams "manly"—not only do both parent strains sound like places you'd go on a year-long trip around the globe during which you'd grow a full beard and get bitten by venomous things a number of times, but the smoke itself, if you believe it, has an aroma of cooked steak. Yes, you read that right; a juicy sirloin just being tossed on the grill for a few seconds before being served up almost raw to a buck hunter with hairy palms. It's that manly. You're going to have to have some hairs on your chest to deal with this stone, too; an incredibly powerful and fairly balanced high that kicks you right in the chest before giving you the sort of right hook that leaves you seeing stars. Hell yeah!

Ninja Turtle

Alright. All you other strains might as well stop trying, because this is the strain for me. A private breeder from the USA named Turtle Man because he carries his home on his back (joke) has invented a cross that references my favorite animated show: the Teenage Mutant Ninja Turtles. Only if a certain type of bud came with free brownies and a bottle of rum would I be more desperate to buy it. A sativa-dominant strain called Ninja Turtle? Take my money, Turtle Man. Please, take my money!

To create this sure-to-please-all-people-who-remember-the-80s strain, the Turtle Man sent some sativa-dominant seeds down in the storm sewers of New York City, where they were lovingly raised and trained in the art of ninjutsu by their older, wiser ratman sensei, Splinter. No, wait; that's wrong. He combined a White Russian plant with a Martian Mean Green plant and stabilized it over several generations. It's easy to get that confused. When the plants started to grow, he named them after Renaissance artists and gave each a different weapon and a different colored mask. The plants grew into Christmas tree-shaped beauties, although they can be bushed out if the grower wishes them to be shorter or wishes to grow them in a SOG set up. This strain is a great one for taking clones from, and the clones will root and grow with great vigor. Although your Ninja Turtle crop will be quite uniform, you may see some differences in personality; for instance, the "Raphael" phenotype will be somewhat more aggressive and testy than his brothers, while the "Michelangelo" pheno will be a lot more laid back and prone to bad jokes. All phenotypes won't be afraid to have your back in a dangerous situation, and although they don't need to be fed often, they will be particularly partial to a good dose of pepperoni pizza every once in a while. After a fairly lengthy flowering period your Ninja Turtles should give you a lot of sass, some ninjutsu training, and an above average yield of beautiful, foxtailing green and orange buds that grow in the shape of a diamond. Disclaimer: I may have confused some of this information with a popular children's cartoon, but I doubt it.

Bred by Turtle Man and Grown by Red Herring, USA

Sativa-Dominant

Genetics: White Russian x Martian Mean Green

If you can ever bring yourself to place such attractive buds into your grinder and roll them into a joint, be prepared for a high that's energetic at first but slides into a narcotic body stone relatively quickly; this isn't a very sativa-style high for very long at all. A little will go a long way; for a few hours at least. Oh, and if April O'Neil comes knocking, you didn't see anything.

OGRE

OGRE from Canada's The Joint Doctor is an incredible strain created by Joint Doctor and a breeder colleague from the UK called Secret Garden Seeds. Comprising genetics from an auto-flowering strain called Secret Circus and a truly exciting Durban Skunk, this is a sativa-dominant auto-flower that exhibits an accelerated growth pattern putting it beyond the height that most auto-flowers reach. If taller plants that need no light cycle change are your thing, get busy learning about OGRE.

The crops of this plant average about 3 feet in height and grow wider than many auto growers might be used to; in fact, if you've only ever grown auto-flowering strains before, this one will give you quite the shock. The vigorous growth waits for no man, and when your seedlings reach the vegetative stage you'll be nothing short of stunned by how quickly they start to build up their side branches. The vegetative stage of this strain is actually extended, and thankfully it's particularly resilient to problems encountered during this time, so if you get too excited and make a huge error, more often than not OGRE won't have a problem getting over it.

Bred by SGS and High Bred Seeds by the Joint Doctor, Canada

Auto-Flowering Sativa-Dominant

Genetics: Secret Citrus (Auto) x Durban Skunk

Potency: THC 15%

jointdoctordirect.com

secretgardenseeds.com

This plant is an extremely heavy feeder so don't be shy with the nutrients, and the breeder recommends using 18 hours of light throughout the whole life cycle for the best results. The recommended set up for OGRE is to grow in 1-gallon pots in a soil-less substrate, up until the point at which the sex is shown around day 21. At this point, growers should transplant into 3-5 gallon pots. After this, the plants will explode and double or even triple their size, then when they flip into flowering they'll set about filling in all the gaps with delicious, succulent-looking buds. After 10 weeks from seed you'll be able to harvest about 80 grams of great bud from each plant.

If you don't think of Shrek when you see these fat buds with hints of ginger (sorry, orange), then you definitely don't live in the same sort of household that I do. Like the inexplicably Scottish children's fantasy star, OGRE is like an onion: it has layers. When it comes to smoking, you'll find that the first layer is a licorice taste with a hint of lime, the second layer is a high that creeps up on you like a kitten stalking its prey, and the third layer is the type of cerebral high that puts you about three feet above everyone else and leaves you up there flying around in the stratosphere like a slightly more ravaged Mary Poppins.

Original Amnesia

The name of this strain from Spain's fantastic Dinafem Seeds seems to be an oxymoron at first, but then as someone who's suffered a few bouts of cannabis-driven amnesia, I can definitely say that your Original Amnesia is the best one of all.

Created by a Hy-Pro, a Dutch breeder, Amnesia is finally being released in its feminized version, which is great news for those who hate throwing away 50% of their seedlings when they turn out to be dudes. Original Amnesia grows more like an indica than a sativa, with a short, relatively bushy structure and a flowering period of just 60

to 70 days. This strain is a heavy producer and the breeders recommend an organic cultivation style to help you get the very best out of your awesome Original Amnesia crop.

Let the name of this strain act as a warning to you; it is incredibly strong. Unless you like waking up under your next door neighbor's porch, wondering how you got muddy knees and a garbage bag full of breadrolls, you'll go easy on this strain and enjoy its seductive stone without letting your brain bleed out entirely! Smoke slowly, folks, you'll want to remember this high. It is lovely.

Dinafem Seeds, Spain

Sativa-Dominant

Genetics: Amnesia by Hy-Pro

Potency: THC 16-22%

dinafem.org

Panama Black

If you're looking for a strain that epitomizes the spirit of Latin America (and aren't we all?), look no further. America's SnowHigh Seeds clearly took the same ill-considered backpacking trip that we all took upon graduating high school, as they've selected some choice genetics from both Panama and Colombia to showcase in this fantastic sativa strain. Panama black was created from two different BCO Black Haze mother plants, which contain both Purple Haze and Colombian Black genetics. Black Haze was then crossed with a Panama Red pheno that exhibited less red traits than its brothers and sisters.

Panama Black expresses a few different phenotypes, which span across the whole spectrum of its genetic makeup. All of these phenos will grow tall, but the Panama Red phenos will grow especially tall and lanky, with many bud sites all along its branches. These will eventually fill out into very dense, resinous flowers, which may mean that the plants need a little assistance in the flowering stage. The Purple Haze phenos yield large, incredibly purple buds that look like they're crusted in sugar; along with their diamond shape and this glittering crystal covering, your buds look like they could be stuck on a gold band and sold. Some phenotypes will exhibit recessive red traits, making them look just like the Panama Reds from the 60s and 70s. The SnowHigh breeders

SnowHigh Seeds, USA

Heirloom Sativa Hybrid

Genetics: Black Haze x Panama Red

strongly recommend using a well-balanced, organic soil for this strain and they advise that re-potting can help to control height for those growers who don't want their Panama Black crop to grow too high and wild. Otherwise, you can expect your plants to stretch two or three times their size once they enter the flowering cycle. Don't fertilize this plant in the way you would other hybrids, as this can actually stunt production and give you disappointing yields in the long run. Experienced growers will know how to get the very best out of this strain in all its expressions, and a good degree of patience will be needed to last out the 12-14 week flowering period. If you provide your Panama Black plants with lots of light and a fair bit of root space, you'll rake in a heavy harvest and your buds will be frosted with the kind of white coating that leaves stoners licking their lips!

Aromas of aged red wine, wood, and earth will tickle your nose when you cure Panama Black buds properly, although some phenos will be sweeter and some even smell like lemon grass. The highs vary in the same way, but all will give you a potent high that can be trippy, intense, and long lasting without all the paranoia that usually comes with these things. An absolutely gorgeous strain.

PHOTOS BY SNOW

Peptide

Over here at Oner Towers we love our buddies from the Great White North, and I'm always stoked to be able to feature new seed companies from upwards of the border. I originally thought that Peptide was produced by the RCMP (the Mounties) because I didn't have my reading glasses on and I was quite mashed; it turns out that this strain is actually an original from Limestone City Seeds, who are part of the Royal Canadian Marijuana Collective. Not the Mounties. And there I was cuing up my Due South DVD and ordering some poutine. There's a lot to be excited about even if Diefenbaker isn't included, though; these guys have over 15 years growing and breeding experience and access to some great genetics, as well as a passion for creating great indoor strains. Canada, you've done it again!

Peptide is an interesting mix of three particular plants; Durban Poison, Heavy Duty Fruity, and a Sweet Tooth #3. The Mom plant was an especially monstrous plant with huge nugs that could knock a man dead, while the Dad plant was a little smaller and more restrained but could still yield with the best of them. The

Limestone City Seeds from the Royal Canadian Marijuana Collective, Canada

Sativa-Dominant

Genetics: (Heavy Duty Fruity x Sweet Tooth #3) x Durban Poison

Potency: THC 16%

rcmcollective.ca

offspring of these two will grow in a Christmas tree shape with a little stretch, so indoor growers will do well to keep the lights close to their plants to avoid them becoming too big. This isn't a huge plant, though; it will reach about medium size and won't cause too much fuss. You can grow Peptide both indoors and out, as it will yield heavily in either situation. Even if you're in one of the colder parts of Canada, you should be fine growing this strain outdoors over the summer months, although you should be careful if your area has particularly cold night times; this strain is a sativa dominant one and they don't tend to handle extended cold periods too well. Stake your plants in the vegetative period so that they don't succumb to the weight of their buds in the middle of the flowering period. Outdoors, your Peptide plants will be ready for harvest around the end of September, whilst indoor growers can bring down their crop between 8 and 9 weeks after forced flowering. Either way, your harvest will be a heavy one, and your Peptide buds will be glittering in the light like a disco ball thanks to the resinous, crystal covered Dad plant. Hooray!

If you can ever bring yourself to break up the huge, gorgeous colas that grow on this plant, your fat, tight Peptide nugs will smell like sweet citrus and cotton candy and the smoke will be the kind that massages your insides as you inhale.

Pineapple Fields

This sounds like a song that should have been on the Sgt. Pepper album, but in fact it's a great sativa-dominant hybrid from Tao of Seeds—and I'm not using the term "great" lightly on this one. In fact, Pineapple Fields is borne of two incredible parent strains, Kali Snapple and Ms. Universe #10. Kali Snapple comes down the family line from pre-2000 Kali Mist crossed with a Snowbud, whilst the male parent, Ms. Universe #10, has another dose of Kali Mist genetics with a good helping of Starship as well. Cross a stinky plant with a medicinal plant and what do you get? A little tree that's dank as all hell.

Pineapple Fields will take to outdoor grows, indoor grows, and greenhouse grows equally well, and will bloom in 11 weeks unless you get lucky with your phenos and get pheno #4, the fast blooming phenotype that finishes in just 58 days. With varying heights, colors, and attitudes, these phenos present a non-uniform crop, but one thing's for sure: They'll all kick out some serious funkiness so make sure you get some charcoal air filters!

Tao of Seeds, USA

Sativa-Dominant

Genetics: Kali Snapple x Ms. Universe #10

taoofseeds.com

Between the fruity smoke and the nice high with its cerebral effects, this strain harks back to 70s Hawaiian pot that made everyone fall in love with each other and walk around naked listening to Zeppelin. It's totally radical, dude.

Pink Genghis

America's Hawaii-based Malama Aina Seeds have taken one of the most beautiful recent cannabis plants and crossed it with a blue classic to create this strain, and damn, has it paid off! A cross between a Blue Ghengis and the wonderful, explosively-colored Redd Cross from Genetics Gone Madd, Pink Ghengis is the sort of strain you could wrap in paper and give to your grandmother. It is the cutting edge of the modern Hawaiian breeding scene.

Balanced between indica and sativa but expressing more sativa growing characteristics, Pink Ghengis is small enough to be grown indoors without much trouble. It feeds heavy and doesn't easily experience nutrient burn, so push your boundaries a little with this strain and see what she can take; it could improve your final yields, so why not see what she can put up with? Topping your Pink Ghengis crop is always a good idea, and she loves aerated soils. Towards the end of flowering, there'll be hints of pink, purple, and even blue, so take in the glorious sight of your grow room before you go in for the chop!

An organic grow will really bring out the gorgeous flavor of this strain; imagine a bowl of fresh berries topped with sugar and cream and you're just about there. The high is a mind-expanding one with enough body buzz to keep you nice and relaxed.

PHOTOS BY GELSTON DWIGHT

Malama Aina Seeds, USA

Sativa-Dominant

Genetics: Blue Genghis x Genetics Gone Madd's Redd Cross

Polm Gold

It's always great to spread the wings of this strain guide series a little further, so I'm thrilled to be able to include a Polish company in this volume. The land of hardworking, friendly folks and my all-time favorite vodka (Zubrowski, if you're asking) is often over-looked in the cannabis community, even the one in Europe, so it's great to be able to represent Poland in these pages! Created by Spliff Seeds in Holland and grown out by Poland's Satindi Seeds, Polm Gold is a truly fascinating mix of some rare genetics. Its three parent strains are Viking, Early Pearl, and an enigmatic strain called Moroc-can Chefchaouen, which is exactly the sort of word you knew existed last time you were playing Scrabble. That's a 25-pointer right there. Nerd? Me?

It might sound like the name of a new Muppet with culinary expertise, but Chefchaouen is actually a region in the Northwest of Morocco from which the original Sativa of this parent strain came. This offspring has been stabilized through many gen-erations, meaning that your crop of Polm Gold should only express one phenotype. It also means that this former heat loving plant is now a fan of European climates and will grow beautifully even in re-gions that experience extreme temperature drops and huge downpours. This plant is not at all suitable for indoor growing, as it is far too tall and far too leggy. Outdoors, however, she'll truly love the space given to her and it will seem like she's never going to stop growing. Polm Gold exhibits phenomenal root growth and will lay down great foundations even on rocky soil. Easily reaching 12 or 13 feet in height, this strain is something of a wild one and as such, requires more than a little experience to really cultivate it properly. Sativa growers will really enjoy the challenges that this strain throws at them, but new growers might find themselves over-whelmed by it. Clones will flower in 2-3 weeks when put under 24 hours of light. Polm Gold crops will be uniform, and will enjoy a vegetative period of 8 weeks before being flipped into flowering. If planted in late May, these plants will be ready for harvest around the middle of September, and should bring in up to 600 grams of bud per plant.

Satindi Seeds, Poland, created by Spliff Seeds, Holland

Sativa-Dominant

Genetics: Moroccan Chefchaouen x Viking x Early Pearl

Potency: THC 17%

satindi.eu

spliffseeds.nl

Be ready for a bit of a shock when you spark up these buds, as they taste like Blueberry and are sweeter than apple pie. Hints of earth and citrus fruit come through on the exhale, and the high is exceptionally strong, being trippy and stoney all at the same time. This is not a strain to miss!

Princess Haze

TreeTown Seeds have been growing, breeding, and loving cannabis for nearly 20 years in their native USA, and in that time they've amassed both some amazing skills and some gorgeous genetics. For this Princess Haze strain they've combined a Princess pheno of a Cinderella 99 plant with Original Haze, resulting in a strain that certainly doesn't need any help with her glass slipper because she's too busy getting hella baked.

A very balanced strain with just a little sativa dominance, Princess Haze will only grow to a few feet in height and won't cause too much havoc in your grow room as long as you have a moderate amount of space. In fact, this is one of the easier sativa-dominant strains to grow, as it enjoys a good resistance to most pests, and yields heavy even in small spaces. Once you've kicked this strain into flowering it will take only 65 days to fully mature, and at the end of that time you'll have orangey-red covered buds in large colas. Expect a great harvest!

The flavor of Princess Haze lingers between berries, apples, and a spicy fuel taste from the Haze. Soon, though, your brain will be hijacked by the incredibly strong and powerful high that seems to keep getting higher and higher. This strain will take you wherever you want to go! For Star Wars fans, this strain reminds me of Princess Leia, and that is a very good thing.

TreeTown Seeds, USA

Sativa-Dominant

Genetics: Cinderella 99 (Princess Pheno) x Original Haze

Potency: THC 15-20%

treetownseeds.com

Psycho Killer Bubba Kush

America's Riot Seeds must be Talking Heads fans to name this cross between BCGA's Killer Queen and a Pre-98 Bubba Kush after the band's 1977 tune Psycho Killer. For this, I want to take them out for a beer and talk about the genius of David Byrne over a toke of this fantastic sativa-dominant bud.

With G-13 and Cinderella 99 in its family tree, it comes as no surprise that this plant is a heavy yielder, and its buds are so resinous that you'd be a fool not to make hash from them. This strain is one that only likes to be grown indoors, and it can finish completely in 67 days of flowering, making it a killer plant for those with indoor grow spaces looking for an excellent sativa to try out. She produces excellent medium to heavy yields of dense, tight buds—just like those of her Bubba Kush parent strains. Seeds of this plant are rare, so don't let them slip by! Sign up for the RiotSeeds.nl forums and keep your eyes peeled for whenever they release a new batch of these killer beans.

The tropical flavors of Psycho Killer Bubba Kush will excite your tastebuds and leave you desperately wanting a pina colada, but hang back on the drinks and let the balanced high take you wherever you want to go. It will hang somewhere between your body and your brain, letting you take control of your experience. Go with it and enjoy yourself!

PHOTOS BY RACERX

Riot Seeds, USA

Sativa-Dominant

Genetics: BCGA Killer Queen x Pre-98 Bubba Kush

Potency: THC 21%

riotseeds.nl

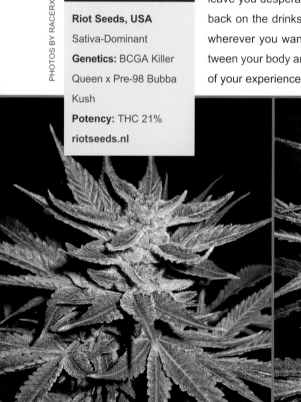

Punto Rojo x Deep Chunk

Garru, the enigmatic but incredibly talented breeder from Spain, definitely doesn't like to do things by halves. In fact, he prefers to do them by thirds; in this case, one third Panama, one third Punto Rojo, and one third Deep Chunk! The old saying "the sum is greater than the parts" has never been more relevant, as this is a unique and fascinating strain that surpasses all of its constituent genetics. It's also a veritable melting pot of cannabis DNA, with the Deep Chunk hailing largely from Afghanistan, the Punta Rosa hailing from Colombia and Panama hailing from that weird isthmus of a country where all the drugs come through. Just kidding. I love Panama. The rum is really cheap there.

Such diversity in genetic history means that this strain could teach us all something about racial harmony, so I suggest we all get blazed on this sativa-dominant beauty and hug it out. Although this plant is a definite hybrid (and proud of it!), there's a lot of purity in its parentage; Panama and Punto Rojo are both pure sativas, whereas Deep Chunk is a pure indica. What does this mean? Well, it means that we're dealing with some stellar genetics for a start. Also, in terms of growing style and smoke, it means that things will be somewhere in the middle, with a plant that leans towards a lankier, taller shape with medium-sized, gently serrated leaves. The flowering time sits around 9 or 10 weeks, which is pretty damn fast for a sativa-dominant plant, and you can expect the resulting buds to be utterly gorgeous, pretty damn stinky, and of medium density. This means that you really don't have to worry about bud rot, but you are going to have to display some patience while you wait for them to become fully ripe.

Breeder Garru, Spain

Sativa-Dominant

Genetics: (Panama Pink Hair x Punto Rojo) x Deep Chunk

Potency: THC 17-19%

The best thing about hybrids, in my humble opinion, is that they can hit that perfect spot between crushing stone and insane high that you're really looking for when you're going about your daily business. This strain is the epitome of that trait, with a high that has a little of the body buzz we all love but is predominantly cerebral, bringing a lot of energy and plastering a smile to your face so you can make your way to work and run your errands without slobbering all over yourself and your computer keyboard. These are the kinds of strains that get us through the day without seeming like complete idiots. For this, Garru, we say thank you!

Pure Africa
(AKA The Resinator)

The Original Sensible team knows a thing or two about growing and breeding pot (okay, a thing or twelve). Of course, when you've spent your life upsetting the establishment and growing and breeding massive amounts of top-quality cannabis, your stories are always going to be entertaining, but the these guys take awesome to a whole new level. They also do the same with their plants, and Pure Africa is a strain that's sure to stop even the most cynical marijuana cultivator in his or her tracks. A pure sativa landrace variety strain from Kenya, Pure Africa may not be a perfect strain for those with only a little growing experience under their belts, but landrace growers and cannabis connoisseurs will fall at the feet of this God-like strain and beg to be allowed to grow it.

As legend has it, Pure Africa was originally plucked from the shadows of Africa's highest peak, on the Kenyan slopes of Mount Kilimanjaro. As a landrace strain it has a fairly wild nature, but it will still thrive in a greenhouse grow set up. However, the breeders really recommend that you grow this strain outdoors in the great wide open where it can flourish to its heart's content. Incredibly resilient to mold and tall as you can imagine, this strain can truly hold its own in a wide variety of environments. After just a 70 day flowering period, which should mean harvest around the middle of November, you'll be straining to reach her huge, delicious looking buds to bring in your phenomenal yield.

Original Sensible, Spain

Pure Sativa

Genetics: Landrace

Kenyan Sativa

Potency: THC 18%

originalsensible.com

Whilst your finished Pure Africa buds will be of a more loose structure that's typical of sativa plants, they'll be dripping with resin like the dankest indica and so sticky that you might have to wear gloves to hold them. The smoke tastes of citrus fruit with a little spice, and the resulting high is nothing short of trippy as hell. It's been said that Kenyans use this strain in religious ceremonies to get themselves to the correct psychedelic frame of mind, and allegedly they also smoke this strain before they go hunting in order to evoke a very concentrated and intense mental state. Closer to home, I've heard it said that if you smoke this plant while watching the Lion King for the 200th time you can get into a semi-hallucinatory state in which you find yourself quoting Hamlet while roaring like Mufasa or screaming about Banquo's ghost while pretending to be wise old Rafiki. To each their own.

Cannabis Sativa The Essential Guide to the World's Finest Marijuana Strains, Volume 3

Pure Gooey

Pure Gooey is a fantastic strain from a private breeder in the USA who developed her for over 30 years. As the name suggests, Pure Gooey was bred from a number of pure strains—namely those from Thailand, Mexico, Cambodia, and Colombia—as well as the kickass 1972 Maui from the original, Asian-based developer. After many trials and tribulations over a 12-year period (including one grow that got eaten by a lucky cow) this combination eventually gave birth (after being cubed with the old SSSC S1) to the Pure Gooey that we know and love today.

A tall plant that particularly loves to be grown outside (but safely away from any errant cows), Pure Gooey is very sativa-dominant and will have the growth patterns of a strong sativa with the compact buds of an indica. Fans of landrace strains will find this a very interesting plant to cultivate, and the breeder recommends a grow set up that's 100% organic. After a lengthy flowering period of 8-10 weeks, you'll be able to harvest a lot of bright, diamond-like buds that are just packed with crystals!

Gooey Breeder, USA

Sativa-Dominant

Genetics: (Cambodian (70s Landrace) x Mex Gold (70s Landrace) x Lumbo Gold (70s Landrace) x Thai (80s Landrace) x 1972 Maui Wowie) x SSSC S1

breedbay.co.uk

cannabisseedauction.com

Pure Gooey is a very strong strain, with its happy sativa high giving way to a body buzz after a few hours. Expect a tingly numbness in your face and a taste of grape flowers with hints of lemons and spicy hash to carry you into your killer high.

Purple Haze Thai

Although "Purple Haze Thai" could be the chapter in my biography that documents three weeks spent backpacking around South East Asia when I was 21 and quite literally empty of common sense (like a cravat-style neck adornment with Jimi Hendrix on it), it is, in fact, a hell of a plant from the wonderful ACE Seeds, who work out of Spain. My theory that it's impossible for any Spanish breeders to kick out a strain that's anything less than amazing certainly isn't being tested by this gorgeous, colorful blend of Purple Haze and Meo Thai F3 genetics, as this plant offers the sought-after Purple Haze characteristics in their most extreme expression.

This 100% sativa variety is one that seriously deserves some attention. A stabilized hybrid of a number of sativas dating right back to the 70s, meaning that you could give some of this to your mom and she'd probably flip right back into being the "happenin' cat" she was back then. This plant grows just as a sativa should; tall and lanky, with branching that does whatever the hell it wants to do. Despite the thin structure,

ACE Seeds, Spain

Pure Sativa

Genetics: Purple Haze x Meo Thai F3

Potency: THC 15%

aceseeds.org

though, this plant has some guts, and its flexible stems will allow it to withstand a multitude of batterings from harsh weather. This plant also enjoys a fairly unbelievable resistance to botrytis, as if it was bitten by something when it was younger and mutated into some botrytis-killing superplant over time. Its size and tendency to branch outwards means that, for most, an outdoor grow will be more practical when growing Purple Haze Thai, but if you can grow indoors, the breeders recommend keeping this plant for breeding or seed production. Outdoors, this strain needs tropical climates to reach its very best, although it can be grown well and comfortably in warm, coastal areas between latitudes 20° and 35°. If you choose to grow outside these latitudes, you might want to pop your plants into a greenhouse for the flowering stage; it will help.

After a long 16-20 week flowering period (hey, this is a 70s-era sativa after all), you'll be desperate to cut down those beautiful purple buds, and I don't blame you. The yields from this strain are decidedly average, but the quality is so phenomenal and hard-hitting that even a medium-sized stash should last you a while. The smoke tastes of blackberry bubblegum and liqueur, but this is nothing compared to the high. Extremely cerebral and massively psychedelic, you'll feel like you stepped into one of those anti-drugs PSAs, like the Thundercats episode where Tygra talks to a female plant then trips balls whilst flying around with massive pupils. Now, please excuse me while I kiss this guy.

Purple Paro Valley

Holy mackerel, this is one beautiful plant. Somebody give Mandala Seeds a shot at this year's Turner Prize, because if that isn't a work of art, then I don't know what is. If you can believe it, the Audrey Hepburn of cannabis over there was in fact bred from a landrace plant from the Paro Valley in Bhutan, and instead of looking like Mowgli on a bad day, it looks like Angelina Jolie after a make over. Good job, guys!

A medium-sized plant that can only really be grown outdoors, this incredibly rare strain may look fragile, but it can withstand the ravages of an outdoor environment way better than you or I might. Purple Paro Valley can withstand both high humidity and extreme drops in temperature, and its resistance to mold is impressive. These plants don't need a lot of nutrients at all, and respond very well to Low Stress Training. In hot climates they can grow to 6 or 7 feet even in containers, and will yield very heavily.

These buds look like they've been covered in Velcro and then rolled in field of heather. Veins of purple run through valleys of green, so gorgeous you barely dare to touch them. Don't let these beautiful good looks fool you; Purple Paro Valley is extremely potent and will have you flying above the clouds before you know it!

Mandala Seeds, Spain

Sativa-Dominant

Genetics: Bhutanese Landrace (Paro Valley)

Potency: THC 8.7-11% / CBD 0.14%

mandalaseeds.com

Purpurea Ticinensis

I could be wrong, but I'm pretty sure I had a bad bout of Purpurea Ticinensis back in high school after that incident with the bottle of moonshine and the rabid ferret, but that could have been something else. Regardless, Switzerland's Owls Production also have a sativa-dominant variety of the same name, so it's only right that I should include that strain in this book. Their breeding stock has been sourced from many different countries, and they're particularly interested in working with strains from their homeland, like the Oldschool Swiss Sativa that mothered Purpurea Ticinensis. This plant has been worked with by the breeders at Owls since 1988, and was allegedly received from some old German ladies in a mountain village who had grown it for decades in their garden. Almost 25 years in the hands of Owl has made it so much more than a decorative plant! It is designed for high altitude growth—like in the mountains, you know?

If you really want to do justice to those Swiss German women, you'll grow Purpurea Ticinensis outdoors (and preferably in Europe), but as we can't all be in the land of amazing trains and even better beer, this strain can also be grown indoors in almost any climate. Those growers looking for the biggest possible yield will want to grow outdoors, although this plant will give a heavy harvest wherever it is cultivated. Some growers recommend starting Purpurea Ticinensis indoors and then transferring into good organic soil outdoors around late March, although transplanting should be done with care so as not to stress the plants any more than necessary. These plants will be medium to tall (and especially tall outdoors) and you'll see purple stripes on the stems right from the vegetative period. You might see some genetic distortions on the leaves, but this is normal for this plant. Regardless of whether your crop endures cold weather or not, the purple of the stems will be carried over into the delicious-looking lilac buds, which will be pale green and littered with bright purple hints. The plants will enjoy good resistance to mold as well as a relatively short flowering time, with outdoor crops being ready for the chop around the beginning of September and indoor crops taking 5-6 weeks.

Owls Production, Switzerland

Sativa-Dominant

Genetics: Oldschool Swiss Sativa

Potency: THC 15%

If Swiss-German mountain women love this plant for its looks and smells, you know that it's got to be special. Your dried Purpurea Ticinensis buds, as well as being a beautiful color, will smell of fruit and chocolate with a strange vegetable smell, too. This strain is a potent one with a nice balanced high, perfect for daytime use, but it also won't keep you up all night if you smoke later in the evening.

Red Headed Stranger

Tierra Rojo Genetics (AKA TR Seeds) by Tierra Rojo, a Texan breeder who relocated to Colorado for the sole reason of growing pot, burst onto the scene in a hail of fresh hash and giant fan leaves a few years ago with this strain, a cross between William's Wonder and Tom Hill's Haze that turned some serious heads in the U.S. cannabis scene. Since then, he hasn't stopped, and Red Headed Stranger has become a firm Colorado favorite.

Bred along with a breeder friend of Tierra Rojo named Paco, this is a strain for true sativa lovers. Tall and strong, this will be a very uniform crop that grows in the same manner as the Haze parent. Your Red Headed Stranger plants will grow vigorous and hardy, without succumbing to mold or infestations easily. Go easy on the nutes and, if possible, grow in an organic soil environment. The Tierra Rojo Genetics grow rooms are beautiful palaces of perfect growing, so don't ruin this strain by putting it into a dodgy hydro system that hasn't been cleaned properly. Red Headed Stranger runs quite long, finishing in between 80 and 100 days, but the wait is most definitely worth it.

True sativa lovers should be flocking to Colorado to buy this soaring, energetic, creative high that gives you a rush like too much coffee but without any of the shaking.

PHOTOS BY RY PRICHARD/KINDREVIEWS.COM

Tierra Rojo Genetics, USA

Sativa-Dominant

Genetics: William's Wonder x Tom Hill's Haze

Potency: THC 17%

facebook.com/TRSeeds

Ringo's Sour Diesel

There you were thinking that Ringo was just the worst Beatle; well, he proved you wrong. He's actually a killer breeder with America's SoHum Seeds. What? It's a different guy? I won't believe it. Only the voice behind the Fat Controller could think of combining Sour Skunk #1 and Sour Diesel to make the fantastic Ringo's Sour Diesel!

Indoor growers are going to love this plant, as it's a medium tall, fat variety that grows bushy and beautiful and finishes in just 8 weeks of flowering. There's some stretch here, so outdoor growers might find themselves with a bit of a monster, but indoors this isn't a problem. What will be a problem, though, is the smell; with so much Skunk involved there's bound to be a whole bunch of odor making its way through your vents. Get some charcoal filters involved and no one gets hurt. Good looking buds will form an average-to-high yield, and they'll be danker than hockey shorts after the playoffs.

The high of this strain will come roaring at you like a steam train through a tunnel, hitting you right at the back of your mind and taking over from there. As soon as the sour smoke clears you'll feel yourself levitating a few feet above the floor, and it will take several hours and at least one viewing of Dazed and Confused to bring you back down to earth.

SoHum Seeds, USA

Sativa-Dominant

Genetics: Sour Skunk #1 x Sour Diesel

Potency: THC 21%

southernhumboldtseed collective.com

Rio Negro Colombian Sativa

Hold on to your hats, folks, because this is a brand new strain that's only just being released by the talented and super lovely Centennial Seeds company, based out of the U.S.A.

A pure sativa from the northernmost country of South America, this is an equatorial plant that harks back to the glory days of cannabis quality, the 70s. Vigorous growth and a bushy structure mean that this strain will flourish before your eyes, and will go on to flower in just 9 or 10 weeks, which is ridiculously fast for an heirloom sativa variety. Although it will grow best in an equatorial setting, indoor growers can recreate the correct environment to really get the best out of this beautiful plant. The sharp serrated leaves and gorgeous deep green buds with light foxtailing makes this plant picture perfect—so much so that you're barely want to cut it down!

Centennial Seeds, USA

Pure Colombian Sativa

Genetics: Landrace Colombian

centennialseeds.com

The fragrance of Rio Negro Colombian Sativa is full of pine and citrus fruits, and this fresh scent is cut with the darker smells of sandalwood when the buds are set alight. The smoke is a unique one, and the high is very energetic; stimulating and pleasing, it's a true keeper!

Ripper Haze

Ripper Seeds, from Spain, are very aware that their native Europe is a hotbed of awesome cannabis genetics right now, and, in fact, they found this "diamond" of a strain on one of their trips to Holland back in 2002. From the genetic line of Amnesia, Ripper Haze is known under several different names; you might have heard it called Amnesia Haze, and you might have heard that it can fell a rhino in a biker gang in one short toke. And you'd have heard just about right.

Both indoor and outdoor growers can experience the fun of growing this strain, as it's a medium tall plant that doesn't bring about too much in the way of complications, even for relatively inexperienced growers. The vegetative stage should run for about 2 weeks, although if you want to keep your plants small you should make this just 1 week. The flowering period will be 60 days or a little more, which translates to mid-October for outdoor growers. This plant is a medium producer, although experienced growers will be able to get a heavy yield from her!

Ripper Seeds, Spain

Sativa-Dominant

Genetics: Amnesia S1

Potency: THC 24%

ripperseeds.com

After a delicious, rich smoke with a very special taste, Ripper Haze gives an almost perfect Haze high—and I don't say that lightly. With an intense aroma, loads of resin, and a long, explosive high, this is some stellar weed.

Rockster's Cheese

This is a strain that will make you feel the way Cheese strains are supposed to make you feel: squinty-eyed and choking with that classic sharp Cheese and Skunk smell. Kaliman Seeds are Cheesemasters—and by that I mean that they love the UK's favorite strain to an extent that might be considered scary, not that they churn their own curds from hand-milked cows (although I don't know; maybe they do). For this strain, they took a cloned 1989 Exodus Cheese strain and crossed it with a Skunk #1. This offspring was then backcrossed three times with the Exodus clone mother. Are you interested yet? You should be.

There's a good reason that the whole of the UK has been gaga for Cheese since the mid 90s; it's damn good pot. It's also a hella fun strain to grow. Rockster's Cheese will show its incredible vigor right from the off, with most seeds popping in just a couple of days; they'll be itching to get into your soil and start laying down some strong roots. With a genetic make up that's mostly sativa, Rockster's Cheese can grow tall when it wants to, but those looking to keep it small will want to flip it into flowering after just 2 or 3 weeks of vegetative growth. Though outdoor growers will just have to let it get as tall as it will, this strain won't top out at much more than 6 feet. Indoors, they'll grow happily and quickly under 18 hours of HPS lighting. The original Exodus Cheese clone exhibited leaves with double serration, and you should be able to see this trait with your Rockster's Cheese crop. If you choose to top these plants they'll react well, but it's not really necessary. They'll grow in the style of a Christmas tree, as most sativas tend to, so there'll be some decent side branching but not a huge amount. When you get to the flowering stage, you better have some damn good ventilation and a shit load of charcoal filters ready, because this crop is going to stink worse than a baby's first poop. I'm talking really stinky. If your neighbors don't notice it, they either have no nostrils or don't clean their cat litter tray out often enough. If you can make it through the heavy dank of your grow room to actually reach your plants, you'll want to harvest after around 67 days of flowering. Wear a nose peg or something. Your eyes will water.

Kaliman Seeds, UK

Sativa-Dominant

Genetics: Cheese x Skunk #1 BX3 (cubed)

Potency: THC 16%

kaliman.co.uk

What can I say about the taste of Rockster's Cheese? It's like a plate of brie and Camembert after a hot day in the sun, cut with a hint of lemon. You can almost chew the smoke, and the high is just as heavy. A must-have for Cheese lovers!

Roots

You can't call your company Reggae Seeds and expect your customers not to think about everything you do in terms of music, so it should come as no surprise to Spain's awesome rasta-styled seed company that I can't help but think of America's greatest hip hop band when I think of this wonderful sativa-dominant strain. Just like its namesake band, this strain comprises some amazing components; although the parent strains are listed as Reina Madre and Kalijah, in reality the family tree of Roots is a lot more diverse and impressive than it first sounds. In fact, the genetics are from the lines of Blue Heaven, NYC Diesel, and a super secretive sativa to name just a few! The breeders at Reggae Seeds worked with the talented Mario from Delicatessen Seeds for this strain, bringing together two absolutely fantastic European companies in one awesome plant.

Thanks to its melting pot (pardon the pun) of fantastic genetics, Roots is a complex little plant with some very interesting traits. If you're growing indoors, your plants (which, obviously, you should name Questlove, Black Thought, Kamal Gray, and Captain Kirk Douglas) won't get too tall at all, as they've inherited most of their growing structure from their Reina Madre parent. However, the sativa can be strong in this one if plants are too far away from the lights and they feel that they have to go for the stretch. Keep your lights as close to the leaves as possible without burning them; put your hands just above the plants, and if you feel a burning sensation on your skin, move the lights further away. As a hybrid, this plant is truly somewhere in the middle of both sativa and indica traits. She is a lot easier to manage than a lot of other hybrids—even newbie growers should find that Roots doesn't cause them as much headache as they might expect. This beautiful little plant has a tendency to foxtail (be still, my beating heart) and, towards the end of flowering, exhibits exactly the kind of colors that Reggae Seeds love; greens, orange-yellows, and reds. Expect huge colas liberally littered with sharp, deep green leaves. Indoor growers can harvest after 60 days of flowering, while outdoor growers should be ready for harvest around the first week of October. Indoors, you can bring in 600 grams per square yard, whilst outdoors, it could be as much as 700. A great yield from a quality plant!

For such a well balanced plant, it comes as something of a surprise that the effect of this delicious smoke is pure sativa; a high-flying, creative, social high that will keep you on your feet and doing things even when your brain is on another planet!

Reggae Seeds, Spain

Sativa-Dominant

Genetics: Reina Madre x Kalijah

Potency: THC 17%

reggaeseeds.com

PHOTOS BY LAJUANNA

S1 (AKA ROOR Nev OS)

Although you might know the name Roor from that mad-looking bong that your friend has that you've always kind of wanted to borrow but were always too afraid of breaking, they're also a Dutch seed company producing exactly the types of strains that befit being packed into a Roor bong. It's as if every time they start creating a strain they ask themselves exactly what would taste delicious while its smoke is barreling up a nice clean glass piece and then playing around your mouth for a few seconds. And isn't that how truly tasty strains are made? This S1, which is also known in some places as Roor Nev OS (not quite as catchy, is it?) was created from a particularly stinky Skunk #1 plant and the original Neville's Haze, and when two of the world's best sativas come along and party you know you're going to have a good time.

As you might expect from the lineage of this plant, it grows tall and thin from the very beginning of its life; even your seedlings will have a good amount of stretch and if you're growing indoors, you're going to have to keep a close eye on how far your lights are from the plants if you want to manage their height. They're like rambunctious children; take your eye off them for 5 minutes and they'll have grown right up to the ceiling or got themselves entwined with the bulbs and be in the midst of getting third degree burns. If you're growing outdoors this incredible vigor should be a help rather than a hindrance. As is the way with sativas, S1 responds incredibly well to natural sunlight rather than HPS light or LEDs, so it will perform better outdoors than in. If you grow indoors, you might find that a SOG or ScrOG system really helps you to get the best out of this crop. Wherever you're growing, you might want to stake your plants as they'll put on considerable girth in the last week of the flowering stage and the slightly leggy branches may struggle to hold the weight of their own buds. This plant isn't one that needs a lot of food to produce its best, and in fact overfeeding can be detrimental to its overall yields. Try feeding with half the recommended amount; this should be perfect for S1. After the 12 weeks of flowering, expect yields up 500 grams per square yard indoors and even more outdoors!

Roor Seeds, Holland

Sativa-Dominant

Genetics: Neville's Haze x Skunk #1

roorseeds.nl

The sweet, Skunky taste of S1 will blow your tastebuds away as it emerges from your quality glass piece, and the sativa high will blow your mind as well; energetic, cerebral, ecstatic, and yet still calming—this is some fantastic quality pot from a great company that isn't afraid to push the envelope when it comes to great genetics.

Sannie's Jack F7

Holland's Sannie's Seeds are like the keepers of the Holy Grail in the cannabis community. If you gather enough tokers together in one of the lounges of an Amsterdam coffee shop, you'll hear hushed whispers and crazy rumors about where they might be in the world and what they might be cooking up next. I've never heard a grower say a bad word about these guys, and their genetics are about as heavily sought after as the Stanley Cup is in Canada. They're held in such high regard in part due to their ballin' genetics and in part due to their almost maniacal dedication to the cause; for their Sannie's Jack F7 strain, for instance, over a decade of work was put into breeding and stabilizing the plant and a very strict selection process meant that only the very best was good enough for the Sannie's breeders. All of that means that this Jack Herer strain is more than your usual Jack.

The goal with this strain was to create a very stable and special Jack Herer, and by God, would you guess that they've achieved just that. There may be some minor variations in the length of the flowering period, but for the most part your Sannie's Jack F7 crop will be very uniform and very impressive looking. These plants won't grow so tall as to rule out indoor cultivation. Your plants will reach 3 feet in height after only a week of vegetative growth, which can alarm some indoor growers without a lot of space as the plants require at least a month of vegetative growth before they're ready to flower. To maximize the use of your space, the breeders recommend growing no more than 9 plants and cultivating them in a SOG set up. You can expect your plants to grow into a very sativa-like shape and style, with lots of side branching, and the flowering time is one that's very common to a lot of sativa-dominant strains, running from anywhere between 10 and 13 weeks indoors. The payoff from this extra long maturation time is that the yields will be incredibly heavy; expect to bring in 750 grams per square yard of grow space, with pale green and white buds, covered in crystals, that smell like lemon candy with hints of Haze.

Sannie's Seeds, Holland

Sativa-Dominant

Genetics: Jack Herer

Potency: THC 22%

sanniesshop.com

Within seconds of toking on Sannie's Jack F7 you'll finally understand what all the fuss is about. The spicy Haze taste will give way to an aftertaste of citrus, and the incredibly powerful Hazey head high will rush into you like a teenager knocking you over with his bike. This is fantastic work from a truly great breeder who consistently releases strains that recreational and medical users alike adore. If you like growing cannabis then you really need to try one of Sannie's strains. You won't regret it.

Santa Muerte

The Spanish-speaking cannabis lovers amongst us will already know that the name of this strain translates to "the Saint of Death" or "Holy Death" but the dark, bleak title of this sativa-dominant hybrid might come as a shock to those who thought it might have been named after some forgotten beach in California that only the surfers know about. In fact, this plant is named as such for its Mexican heritage, as many Mexican Catholics consider the Holy Death to be an integral part of their belief systems, which also encompasses the incredibly famous Day of the Dead (Dia de Muertos) and those wicked-cool sugar skulls that all the emo kids like to wear these days. Spain's Blimburn Seeds clearly know their Latin American culture!

The result of a Mexican sativa and an Original Haze plant that hung out for a while and eventually made it past the friend zone, Santa Muerte is a big beast, reaching 9 or 10 feet outdoors and producing between 500 and 600 grams of high-quality bud when harvest comes around. It's very traditionally sativa in the way that it grows and flowers, with leggy branching and a structure that is more flexible than strong. Most growers will find it easier to grow this plant outdoors, as it needs quite a lot of space in which to flourish and indoor growers might struggle to give it as much room as it needs. Outdoor growers will find it to be stable, if in need of a little love every now and then (but really, aren't we all?). Although the vegetative period is relatively short and full of growth, the flowering period is around 75 days, which is relatively long but in the usual range for a sativa-heavy hybrid. Towards the end of the flowering period you'll start to realize why the Blimburn breeders might have decided to christen this plant with such a sinister handle; the buds, nearing the end of their lives, become a deep, dark green color and start to look decidedly spooky. I recommend chopping them, trimming them, and drying them out before they start to freak out the rest of the plants.

BlimBurn Seeds, Spain

Sativa-Dominant

Genetics: Mexicana x Original Haze

Potency: THC 16%

blimburnseeds.com

Once you've got your dried and cured buds safely contained in glass jars where they can't frighten anyone, you can go right ahead and send them to their smoky death. The unmistakable smell of the Haze parent will cut right through the air, and you'll recognize that spicy taste before the very, very cerebral high takes over and you start thinking about sugar skulls and dead saints all over again. When you're at the peak of your high, I suggest putting on the Muppets and eating vanilla ice cream. These things are decidedly less scary.

Satori

Spain's Mandala Seeds never cease to impress me with the range of genetics that they work with, and this strain shows yet another of the gems from their seed stock; namely, a Nepalese sativa with some fantastic medicinal effects. They crossed this beauty with a super secret strain to produce Satori, which shares its name with the Japanese Buddhist word for "awakening." You certainly will be awakened by this strain!

Flowering in just 70 days whether it's indoors or out, Satori performs well under 600 watts of HPS lights per square yard in a grow room. It's a slim plant that won't grow beyond medium height, but she's very resistant to mold and is especially good at fending off spider mites. Her side branches give excellent cuttings for cloning, and she'll barely need feeding if you use quality soil and let her do her thing. Expect harvests along the lines of 600 grams per square yard indoors or a phenomenal 1200 grams per plant outdoors.

These fruity, slightly spicy buds will be ridiculously resinous after the chop, and only a fool would pass up on making the kind of Nepalese Temple Balls that this plant can give you. There's no finer hash to be had, and whether you're smoking the resin or the buds, this strain will floor even the most hardcore of tokers.

Mandala Seeds, Spain

Sativa-Dominant

Genetics: Nepalese x Unknown

Potency: THC 23-28%

mandalaseeds.com

Serious 6

Holland's Serious Seeds have leaped into the world of landrace African strains for their Serious 6 strain, but rather than going down the well-trodden path of pairing this with a Kush or a Haze, they've gone a little further north and have chosen a secret Canadian strain to be its mate. The resulting plant is a fast flowerer and enjoys a massive resistance to mold. Serious Seeds spent years developing this strain, and it was definitely worth the wait.

Outdoors, Serious 6 grows tall and thin as it is an almost pure sativa, although indoor growers can stunt this height to suit their needs. This plant prefers colder environments that are incredibly humid, and in such a climate they'll be fully finished by the end of September. Indoors, the flowering time sits at around 58 days, and clones will grow in 10 days or less. The beautifully resinous and purple-tinged buds will be in abundance, and you should take in around 500 grams per square yard of grow space.

The smoke of Serious 6 is much like sticking your hand into a candy jar and shoving everything into your mouth at once; you'll get sweet citrusy flavors, licorice, spicy tartness, and even a little earthy taste. The effect is much like a sugar high, too; creative, powerful, all cerebral, and the sort of high that makes you unbearable to be around because you just can't sit still!

PHOTOS BY GREEN BORN IDENTITY

Serious Seeds, Holland

Sativa-Dominant

Genetics: Landrace African Sativa x Undisclosed Canadian Strain

Potency: THC 17%

seriousseeds.com

Shaman

Named after a traditional spiritual guide who would take you on a cerebral journey through your own consciousness and stuff, this strain from Holland's Dutch Passion is the sort of smoke that might just change your life. A variety dating back to the 80s, Shaman is a combination of Purple #1 and Skunk genetics bred particularly for the outdoor or greenhouse grower. With a strong sativa dominance, this plant will grow in a gorgeous and classical style even though it won't be the tallest cannabis plant you've ever seen. This is a great strain for sativa lovers that want a relatively easy grow.

Reaching only 5 or 6 feet in height at its tallest, Shaman won't be the most imposing sativa strain in your garden but it might just be the most beautiful. The 25% indica genetics of this strain have worked to tame the sativa stretch somewhat, meaning that greenhouse growers will find Shaman to be almost perfect for their cultivation space. Careful trimming and training of this strain can result in an even bushier structure, although there will be a little stretch in her. Growers will also find that this strain is one of the most hardy plants they've ever cultivated, as it is highly resistant to both spidermites, those eternal enemies of the outdoor grower, and mold. If you live in a particularly humid area, it will be a good idea to watch out for bud rot, even though it's unlikely that this will take hold. Whilst the breeders claim that only about 50% of Shaman plants will turn blue, many Shaman crops end up dark purple with barely a touch of green or white on them. The flowering time of this strain is around 8 weeks, which translates to a harvest date of around the end of September or the start of October outdoors. Whilst this is primarily an outdoor and greenhouse strain, determined indoor growers will find that it can be grown inside, although the plants will be decidedly less impressive and will yield nowhere near as highly as their outdoor compadres. Around harvest time, your Shaman outdoor buds will be dripping with resin and so colorful that you'll be crying when you pull them down. You'll be glad you did, though, when you weigh in your fairly heavy harvest and take in the scintillating aroma of your newest stash.

Dutch Passion, Holland

Sativa-Dominant

Genetics: Purple #1 x Skunk

Potency: 13.7%

dutch-passion.nl

With a typical "purple" taste and a sharp sweetness, the smoke of Shaman is thoroughly enjoyable and well worth a good long curing period. The taste, though, is simply the cherry on top of this fantastic smoke, with the heady, thoughtful, cerebral high being the true pull of this strain. Let this Shaman take you on a path of discovery around your inner self, or alternatively play Cranium with your friends and have an absolute riot.

Sherpa

Sherpa, from Canada's Tight Genes, knows what she's doing. Like all Sherpas, she's from good stock, knows your weaknesses, and can take you to the highest peaks imaginable if you'll just let her. Also like Sherpas, she's a little enigmatic, and although no one will say what her parents are for sure, we can at least believe that she's been working these hills for a good long while and knows just where to take you.

Sherpa goes on a long haul to reach her end point, but the journey there is going to be beautiful, so don't worry too much about the 70 days of flowering time; instead, enjoy the process of growing, as this plant produces gorgeous, thick colas that are frosted to the tips. Like all Sherpas, she can support her own weight, and shouldn't need much assistance even toward the end of the flowering period. The yield of this strain is heavy, sitting at around 600 grams per square yard of grow room, which, ironically, you would probably need a Sherpa to carry if you were bringing it all up a hill from your secret mountain grow.

Tight Genes, Canada

Sativa-Dominant

Genetics: Nepalese Haze

This strain has a fascinating mix of aromas, with star anise, oregano, and flowers all coming into the mix. The extremely strong head high will plant your brain on top of a mountain. It's a good job you have a Sherpa as your guide, as you'll have no damn idea where you are.

Silver Star Haze

Holland's The Bulldog Seeds have had a colorful history in the cannabis community of Amsterdam, and over the years they've become something of a mainstay in the European cannabis scene as a whole. Of course, when someone has become an expert in a certain field it's only right that those with lesser knowledge sit and listen to what the experts have to say, so it's with true excitement that I sit cross legged every time the Bulldog releases a new strain. If I was to guess at what they're trying to say with Silver Star Haze, it would be that if you use truly fabulous cannabis genetics you can in fact create a sativa-dominant strain that can be grown in smaller grow spaces without losing any of its personality or the sativa high that everyone loves. To achieve this, they've combined genetics from three absolutely classic plants: Skunk #1, Northern Lights, and an original Haze. And with that family tree, the community falls silent and listens to the Bulldog!

As Silver Star Haze is a fairly balanced strain with only a little sativa dominance, sativa lovers who don't have much experience cultivating this type of strain might decide that this is a good plant to start on. With a relatively short stature and a brief flowering period, this plant introduces you to sativa cultivation without overwhelming you, while still giving you finished buds that any sativa grower would be proud of. While the plants do grow to a medium tall height, they will grow an in incredibly uniform crop and the main body will be fairly compact and dense. The structure is strong and hardy, and the plants will exhibit a good resistance to mold and mites as long as they're not subjected to an incredibly humid climate.

The Bulldog Seeds, Holland

Sativa-Dominant

Genetics: Skunk #1 x Northern Light x Haze

Potency: THC 19.12% / CBD 0.15%

bulldogseeds.nl

If your grow room is a little too damp, keep an eye on the stalks and also the buds when the flowering period rolls around. The flowering period will be 10 or 11 weeks long indoors, which translates to a harvest at the end of October for outdoor growers. The Skunk influence means that odor control will be very necessary and even outdoor crops will be crazy stinky. This strain is a heavy yielder, so indoor growers can expect to bring in around 700 grams per square yard of grow room, while there's no limit to the huge harvest that can come from an outdoor plant. The sky's the limit!

With a taste that's very Skunk and a taste that's pure Haze, your finished Silver Star Haze buds will be a riot of different expressions. The high, however, is pretty unified: an incredible sativa head effect that sets your mouth talking at a million miles an hour and sets your brain running just as quickly. A great euphoric strain.

Smile

I make no bones about the fact that Kannabia are one of my favorite Spanish seed companies. Their breeders are as fun as they are talented, and I've always dreamed of spending a month in Spain just watching them do their thing. However, if they didn't grow some amazing pot they'd just be nice guys from Spain; thankfully, they are veritable wizards with weed, so we can all go ahead and be super fan-girly about them. Eeeee!

Smile is a cross between an AK-47 that yields like its life depends on it and an Orange Bud plant that tastes like it's just been pulled off a tree in California. The result is an ultra-fast sativa-dominant strain that tastes delicious and gives a mega harvest. Although your Smile crops will look pretty skinny from the outset, they'll open up soon enough, turning from a pine-tree grow style to a bushier specimen. The stems and branches of this strain will be thick and hardy, and over the whole course of its life it will be strongly resistant to mold and attacks from a whole variety of pests, which is great news for anyone that doesn't own barrels of Neem oil. This also means that newbie growers might find this a fantastic choice, as they won't be reaching for their grow books every two minutes when they see some unwanted critters lurking around the area. There are a number of different phenotypes that can be expressed by Smile; some will be more obviously sativa-dominant and some will be smaller and more squat. The more sativa-style plants will enjoy a slightly extended vegetative period of 65 days, while the more indica ones can be flipped after just 56. The breeders recommend ramping up your anti-odor methods right at the beginning of the flowering stage, as Smile is a particularly stinky plant. Although the freshly-blossoming buds will seem quite loose and airy, they'll start to tighten up at around the fourth week of flower and will be dense and stiff by the time harvest rolls around. After about 60 days of flowering your crop should be ready for harvest, and get prepared for a bit of hard work ahead; you should be able to bring down at least 400 grams of quality bud per square yard of grow space.

Kannabia Seeds, Spain

Sativa-Dominant

Genetics: AK-47 x
Orange Bud

Potency: THC 21%

kannabia.es

All through the flowering period your room will smell of cut grass and oranges, but once the buds are cured the smell will become almost overwhelming. The smoke is tangy and fresh, while the high is one that's relaxing with enough energy to keep you awake and enjoying it. For medical and recreational use alike, this is a fantastic, fresh strain that will definitely make you Smile.

Sour Diesel #2

I love me some Diesel, and I'm not afraid to say that I'd probably walk over injured friends and leave my parents stranded on the side of the highway with a flat tire in the middle of winter if I knew I could get some seriously dank Sour Diesel on the go. There's something about that bitter smoke and the heady high that just floats my boat; I can't help it. Thankfully, the Humboldt Seed Organisation recognize what I like to think of as SDAD or Sour Diesel Addiction Syndrome and they spend a lot of time catering to fools like me who just can't get enough of that cruel green mistress. To create this wonderful strain, they've brought together an Original Diesel with the enigmatically-named DNL. DNL, despite its acronym, is actually a combination of RFK Skunk, Northern Lights, and a Hawaiian Sativa. DNL is a fairly legendary strain that people don't know a lot about, but rest assured that its best traits are clearly visible in Sour Diesel #2.

This is a tall plant that performs well both indoors and out, although outdoor growers will find themselves with a greater yield at the end of the growing cycle. A steady stream of nutrients will be beneficial to this strain and it will grow well in most types of systems, although an organic soil grow will be preferable, especially if you're growing for medicinal use. These plants will turn out to be quite bushy for sativas, so be sure that you leave enough space for them to grow horizontally as well as vertically; no one likes it when their plants get a bit constricted. Indoors, Sour Diesel #2 should finish in around 9 weeks, and outdoor growers should be ready to harvest around October 10th in the Northern Hemisphere. Whatever your growing style, your yields will be slightly above average and every single bud will be a star performer once it's in your bong.

Humboldt Seed Organisation, USA

Sativa-Dominant

Genetics: Original Diesel x DNL

Potency: THC 19%

humboldtseeds.co.uk

Every Diesel connoisseur already knows and loves the sharp hints and dull tones of the Diesel family, but this strain adds an earthy, darker taste to the usual flavor, and supertasters might be able to detect a hint of pine, as well. The best thing about this type of strain, though, is the high: clear, sharp, strong, and ridiculously happy, a Sour Diesel #2 high lasts seemingly forever, leaving you skipping off down the street like exactly the kind of idiot that annoys all the 9-5ers. Don't worry though; you'll barely be able to feel their ire as you bounce along the street thinking about rainbows and unicorns and a few of your favorite things.

Sour Power

Holland's Hortilab have been in the game long enough to know what's what, so when they tell you that they have a sister phenotype of their StarBud x East Coast Sour Diesel v3, you sit up and listen. Or, rather, you have a rip on the bong when they pass it around, and three seconds later you admit, through coughs, that they were right.

A complex mix of both indica and sativa genetics with a slight bias to the latter, this strain is a medium-height plant that can be grown in almost any environment. It's best to give these plants a lot of room, but if you only have a small grow room they can be trained to stay to a height that suits your space. When you flip the plants into flower be ready to see some absolutely gorgeous foxtailing on the buds; it makes the green flowers look like something you'd find at the Chelsea Flower Show. Yield is high, so be ready for some hard work come harvest time!

As any Diesel lovers like me will appreciate, this strain gives an incredibly powerful sativa high that will help you be creative, focused, and social all in one go, and that will last long into the night if you need it to. You don't need many tokes on Sour Power to keep flying high, but it's hard not to indulge in a smoke that tastes so good. Another great hybrid from one of the great seed companies working to revitalize the Dutch cannabis scene through highly comprehensive and calculated breeding regimes and short, high quality seed runs.

HortiLab Seed Company, Holland

Sativa-Dominant

Genetics: Sister Phenotype of StarBud x East Coast Sour Diesel v3

Potency: THC 20.5%

hortilab.nl

South Indian

If you've read the other volumes in this series of strain guides (and if not…why not?), you'll already know that AutoFem are a company that I definitely hold in high regard. Specializing in auto-flowering varieties, this Spanish company has carved out a very particular place for themselves in the European cannabis market and they regularly push their own boundaries, improving their commercial strains and their seed stock again and again. South Indian is a great example of the way in which they do this; a non-commercial strain from their pool of genetics, this is a pure landrace strain from India, and if, like me, you're something of a landrace lover, it will seriously blow your mind.

Stabilized over the years by the breeder at AufoFem, this strain has been somewhat calmed by the process but still acts as the cannabis equivalent of Marlon Brando in "The Wild One." It has been used many times in commercial hybrid strains, but as a plant to behold, it's a true beauty. As you would expect from a landrace sativa, it's tall, thin and its branches look like the arms of one of those Wacky Waving Inflatable Arm Flailing Tube Men; they're everywhere. In flowering, South Indian produces long, fluffy buds that aren't too loose and aren't too tight, and enjoy a moderate coating of trichomes; they don't look like they've been dipped in icing sugar, but they have a delicious-looking sheen to them. The buds are pale green and have yellow and white highlights, but really, this is a green plant through and through. If you're lucky enough to get your hands on some of these genetics, your grow room will be awash with scents of pine, mint, and the odd cheeky whiff of incense when harvest time creeps nearer.

AutoFem Seeds, Spain

Pure Landrace Indian

Genetics: Stabilized South Indian Landrace

The tolerance to this plant is non-existent. Seriously. You can be smoking this every day for a month straight, and you'll be flying just as high on day 30 as you were on day 1. Although smoking throughout the day might result in a plateau at some point, the next day it will be as if you never smoked a sativa in your life before. While the high isn't devastating, it is incredibly energetic and clear, making you feel like you stopped at a traffic light and someone cleaned your mental windows; you didn't even realize they were dirty, but now they're clean, you're definitely going to have to tip someone a dollar. The smoke is fresh tasting and smooth, massaging your throat as it goes down, leaving just a hint of a hashy taste on the exhale. All your senses will be sharp as a tack throughout the day, making this an awesome wake 'n bake strain.

South Star

They might be based in Holland these days, but don't you go thinking that the guys and girls behind Kiwiseeds are anything but true New Zealanders. In fact, this seed company was started back in 2002 with the sole purpose of saving and preserving some of the "old school" Kiwi genetics that were once found in the stashes of every self-respecting son of Aotearoa. Worried that these genetics were rapidly disappearing from circulation, the Kiwiseeds breeders sought out the kinds of strains that were everywhere in their homeland in the mid 90s; mainly sativa strains that had been brought over from places like Mexico, Thailand, Vietnam, and India by breeders, growers, and enthusiasts in the 70s. They've since worked with a variety of different plants and genetics; for this South Star strain, they've crossed Haze and Northern Lights to get a gorgeous sativa-dominant plant that their home country would be proud of.

Despite being a Haze cross, South Star only grows to about 3 or 4 feet in most conditions, meaning that indoor growers will have a field day with this strain. It can also be grown outdoors where it might reach a little taller, but this is predominantly a medium-sized plant with a Christmas-tree-like growing structure. Bringing so much sativa in such an indica-like package is no mean feat, and I can only assume that Kiwiseeds will be the seed company of choice for sativa lovers who grow indoors from now on. From the vegetative stage, your South Star plants will look pretty damn classic, and when the flowering stage kicks in your grow room will be awash with green, yellow, and white waves of color. This plant should do well in most climates, especially those that aren't crazy hot and humid; the Dutch climate is pretty much the perfect one for this strain. Huge, fairly loose colas will grow in not much time at all, and your plants will be fully matured and ready for harvest just 70 days after forced flowering. South Star is a medium to heavy yielder, and you can expect to harvest around 400 grams per square yard of grow space, with maybe a little more from an outdoor crop. Be sure to take in the bud as you take them down; they're a beautiful sight to behold.

Kiwiseeds, Holland

Sativa-Dominant

Genetics: Haze x Northern Lights

Potency: THC 16%

kiwiseeds.com

As you might expect from a company that seeks to preserve the very best things about great sativas, Kiwiseeds have made sure that South Star has one hell of a killer high. Although it's a bit of a creeper, this is a very energetic high that, once it's set in, lasts for at least two hours. Add to this the very pleasurable taste and you've got yourself some amazing daytime-smoking pot!

Space Grape

The UK's Ultra Genetics have got a fabulous combination of Nebula and Grapefruit genetics in Space Grape, bringing in their favorite fast-flowering sativa and a Grapefruit indica father to create something really special. This strain promises to give you the best of both worlds—and who are we to argue?

Suitable for both indoor and outdoor cultivation, Space Grape exhibits a more typically indica structure and growth pattern, although lucky outdoor growers might just see it blossom into a sativa-style tree if conditions are right and a long vegetative period is allowed. Even when kept relatively small in an indoor grow room, this plant will be a fun one to grow, as it keeps itself to itself and doesn't require anything special to grow to its potential. Slim, sharp green leaves and dense green buds give away the sativa influence here, but the flowering time sits at a relatively quick 70 days. Expect an above average yield, and those with the rare trees might need some assistance in bringing down their massive harvest!

Ultra Genetics, UK

Sativa-Dominant

Genetics: Nebula x Grapefruit

Potency: THC 18%

ultra-genetics.com

puresativa.com

sativasister.cz

Space Grape enjoys a fruity, berry flavor that's sweet with a little tang. The smoke is smooth and tasty, giving way to a very clear, soaring sativa high that's just the icing on the delicious cake. A fantastic daytime smoke that won't set you down too hard.

Starship

Carrying the torch of the USA cannabis breeding community right into outer space are Dynasty Seeds with their original Starship, a sativa-dominant strain that is just ripe for me to use many 2001: A Space Odyssey puns and jokes about David Bowie. It's also an impressive mixture of Kali Snapple and Pineapple Kush genetics, making it like catnip to American tokers.

A medium-sized plant that grows as well indoors as it does outdoors, Starship enjoys a fast flowering period of just 60 days and displays some good, bushy branching that will impress even dedicated indica growers. You can expect to harvest up to 120 grams of prime bud per plant if they're given enough root space, so growing outdoors can get the very best out of these beauties, and the cold of night will bring out their bright purple hues. Though the aroma when growing is of burnt rubber and gasoline, the smoke will surprise you with its sweet, tangy pineapple flavor and creamy hash aftertaste.

These buds truly look a bit alien, with purple colorings and trichomes that are so turgid they look like those eyes-on-the-ends-of-stalks from 60s drawings of extraterrestrials. This review wouldn't be complete without one cringe-worthy pun, so suffice it to say that this Starship will really send you into outer space! (Groan).

Dynasty Seeds, USA

Sativa-Dominant

Genetics: Kali Snapple x Pineapple Kush

Potency: THC 19%

dynastyseeds.com

Stitch's Love Potion

If, like me, you thought that this strain was going to be a Disney-inspired offshoot of their 2002 alien-makes-good movie, focusing on how Experiment 626 fully adapts to the commercialization of American culture and finally releases his own scent, you're going to be disappointed. However, if you assumed that Stitch's Love Potion was going to be a pretty impressive sativa-dominant strain that included Purple Stitch in its genetic make up—well, you were right on the money. No, this Stitch isn't a genetic experiment gone wrong; he's a French cannabis breeder who has got his hands on some hella awesome breeding stock and more than enough knowledge to know what to do with it. For Stitch's Love Potion, he's bred two of his own strains, Kush Van Stitch and Purple Stitch, with Zamal and Mangobiche, which might not make a lot of sense to you, but just take it from me: it's good news.

Topping out at about 3 or 4 feet, this certainly isn't a very tall plant for one that's sativa-dominant, but this means that it's perfectly designed for an indoor grow or even a small closet grow space, depending on your set up. Stitch's Love Potion can also be grown outdoors, and climates similar to those of Northern Spain will yield the best results. If your area experiences cold snaps in the summer, you might want to grow indoors instead. This is an F1 strain and as such can express various different phenotypes, but none of these will grow particularly tall and all will give a sizable yield by the end of the flowering period. This strain has some great side branching which makes it suitable for SOG and ScrOG techniques, although if you have never tried growing in this way before it might be a good idea to seek out some help; you don't want to mess up this crop, as you'll be losing some fantastic quality bud. All phenotypes flower fairly quickly, and all are fantastic producers; expect a heavy harvest from your crop of Stitch's Love Potion.

Breeder Stitch, Spain

Sativa-Dominant

Genetics: Kush Van Stitch x (Zamal x Mangobiche) x Purple Stitch

Potency: THC 16%

AutoFem by Stitch

flashseedsbank.com

Stitch himself describes this strain as an invitation to come and have a pleasant trip on his intergalactic space love ship, but I think we can put that comment down to watching too many reruns of Austin Powers over huge bowls of Love Potion. Even if you're not keen to go interstellar with Stitch himself, you'll find that this strain gives your libido a nice kick up the backside. Perfect for daytime toking (as long as you can keep yourself from dry humping strangers on the street), this is a smoke full of good vibes that may help those suffering from depression as well as those that just like to feel groovy.

Stonehedge

Holland's Sagarmatha Seeds have been doing their thing in the cannabis community for a long time now, and it's testament to their ability to produce damn good marijuana that they're still here doing what they do best. These guys have a great track record for using excellent genetics, and Stonehedge is no different. For this strain, they've combined a sativa plant from Cambodia with a Western Winds hybrid to create a strain that yields well and grows like a sativa but comes in thick and dense to create tall, stone-thick plants that will remind you of Wiltshire's most famous stone circle!

If you find yourself with some Stonehedge beans in your hand and you're ready to pop them, make sure you're prepared for a damn serious plant and all that comes with it. This is the most dense sativa in the Sagarmatha cannon, and although it only grows to a few feet in height it will fill out like an injured college football player who can't exercise and instead fills the hole in his life with Twinkies. If you're truly dedicated to honoring the name of this strain, you'll grow this strain outdoors, arranged into a circle with one "heel stone" plant outside of the circle. If you're dedicated to the point of insane, you'll erect a chain-link fence around the entire thing and charge people to come and stand behind the fence to look at your arrangement. You'll only take down the fence twice a year, overnight on both Winter and Summer Solstice, when you'll have 10,000 normal people partying around the plants and about 10,000 teenagers on drugs climbing on top of them, whilst Hare Krishnas wander round giving everyone free food. If you do decide to go down this route, be sure to stake your plants so they don't collapse under the weight of a sweaty 17-year-old on ketamine. The strong structure of this strain means that it generally won't need assistance, and you can instead concentrate on keeping an eye out for mold and other pests. Vegetate your Stonehedge plants until you see 4-7 internodes and then force flowering; after this, you'll need to allow for a 65-day flowering period. After this point you will be able to harvest around 350 grams of quality bud per square yard of grow space.

Sagarmatha Seeds, Holland

Sativa-Dominant

Genetics: Cambodian Sativa x Western Winds

Potency: THC 16-18%

highestseeds.com

These Stonehedge buds will be as dense as the center of a black hole and will smell very hashy; in fact, they'll feel so tight and heavy that you'll barely believe they've come from a sativa-dominant plant. However, when the creeper high finally reaches you and gives you a good dose of pure energy along with a nice relaxing body buzz, you'll appreciate the marriage of sativa and indica in this fantastic plant.

Super Lemon Haze

Super Lemon Haze is one of those strains that you lose your mind over when you're a teenager and your "guy," who usually only ever has bagweed that he passes off as "some dope indica from Cali," finally gets in something that you've heard of and read about in the pages of SKUNK Magazine. My mom told me recently that Super Lemon Haze was one of the first types of pot she ever smoked where she could actually taste a distinct flavor, that lemon cutting right through the bullshit of all the other "dank kushes" and giving her something she could really appreciate and understand what the fuss was all about. Green House Seed Company are basically the Jay-Z of the seed world, and this is one of their best strains. And my mom loves it (but she hates hip hop).

Derived from a Lemon Skunk plant and a Super Silver Haze, this strain made quite the splash when it was first introduced and continues to do so to this day. It's a medium plant, meaning that both indoor and outdoor growers can enjoy the experience of cultivating it, although outdoor growers might have the edge in getting the highest yields when harvest rolls around in mid-October. For the indoor grower, this plant can make a fantastic choice for a ScrOG set up thanks to its long, wide branches that take well to being manipulated. It can also be a great crop for those looking to experiment with Low Stress Training. She is not only malleable and robust but she tends to deal well with any stupid rookie errors that you might make along the way. The flowering period is also medium, as Super Lemon Haze finishes in 10 weeks indoors, which will just whizz by for those used to longer-finishing sativas. Towards the end of the flowering period these plants most definitely need some additional support to hold the weight of their intense colas, so be sure to have some stakes ready in the vegetative stage. Indoor growers can look forward to yields of 800 grams per square yard, but it's the outdoor growers who will truly hit the jackpot, raking in up to 1200 grams from each individual plant. I know; make friends with these guys, stat.

Green House Seed Co., Holland

Sativa-Dominant

Genetics: Lemon Skunk x Super Silver Haze

Potency: THC 19.33% / CBD 0.21%

greenhouseseeds.nl

It's not only the gorgeous look of these buds that will send your mouth into a salivation overdrive; the intense lemony smell is also enticing, and when the buds are lit it bursts into a gorgeous flavor right on your tongue. The Hazey aftertaste isn't as intense but it's definitely there as the balanced high sets in, leaving you feeling incredibly social and physically relaxed at the same time. A true modern classic.

Super Sour OG

The Emerald Triangle is a true hotbed of U.S. cannabis genetics, and even on a cold, wintry day in December, you can pretty much smell the dank in the breeze that moves across the hills. Emerald Triangle Seeds know this, and they work hard in promoting top-quality American genetics that could rival any Spanish or Dutch offerings. Super Sour OG is one of these awesome offerings, with genetics from a plethora of amazing North American strains, which pretty much ensures that every dedicated toker north of the equator will be desperate to get their hands on this strain!

Not two, not three, but four fantastic strains comprise this sativa-dominant plant: Blueberry, Sour Diesel, OG Kush, and the fantastic Lost Coast OG. The breeders recommend tying down and training your plants so that they'll eventually grow a number of very uniform colas with as many as 20 connecting internodal sites. With this technique, they say that you can harvest up to 1500 grams from a single plant, which means that your plant must look like Dwayne Johnson when it comes to harvesting time. Regardless of whether you train the plants or not, they will double in size when you switch them from vegetative to flowering, so be sure that you've left enough space for each plant to grow into and that you flip at the right time. The breeders recommend a steady intake of nitrogen in the last few weeks of flowering to help your crop truly reach its potential, but even if this isn't in your budget or growing style, you'll walk away from this crop with the kind of yield that brings tears to the eyes of grown men. Indoor growers will be looking to harvest at the 8th or 9th week of flowering, while outdoor growers in the Northern Hemisphere will be harvesting in the first week of October.

Emerald Triangle Seeds, USA

Sativa-Dominant

Genetics: (Blueberry x Sour Diesel x OG Kush) x Lost Coast OG

Potency: THC 15.69%

emeraldtriangleseeds.co.uk

The taste of this strain, as you'd expect, is overwhelmingly sour with just a hint of sweetness to make it manageable, and a cheeky hint of berries on the exhale. If, like me, you're a fan of Sour strains, it's worth giving your harvested buds a good long curing period to really bring out the kind of flavors that make your face twitch, thanks to the gorgeous bitterness. With such a mix of genetics, it makes sense that the high is a balanced one, but the Super Sour OG high is more than balanced; it's almost perfect. The energetic, carefree beginning eventually mellows out into a relaxed happiness with enough body buzz to make it fun; smoking this is almost like smoking a sativa and then an indica, one after another.

Swazi

Spain's Tropical Seeds Company have pulled out a real corker with this strain, a pure sativa straight from Swaziland, South Africa. This talented set of European breeders must have had a riot when creating this strain; it's a fiery-looking one with gorgeous sativa traits and a high that will send you intergalactic!

Due to its wild nature, Swazi is only really available to outdoor growers, as it simply will not be tamed into an indoor grow room. Growing to 9 feet or more, this is the kind of strain that you just have to let do what it wants, like a teenager that's grown taller than his mom. Thankfully, this strain is shockingly well behaved and doesn't require much attention from its carer, although you should always be on the watch out for buds and pests. Swazi is incredibly resistant to disease and flowers surprisingly early for a pure sativa. Your harvest should be planned for around September 15th if you're growing around 40 degrees latitude. You should pull in around 500 grams of fantastic sativa bud per plant when the flowering time is over.

Tropical Seeds Company, Spain

Pure Sativa

Genetics: Landrace Swaziland Sativa

Potency: THC 14%

tropicalseedscompany.com

Sweet as a slice of pie with extra ice cream, Swazi is an absolutely delicious smoke—but that's nothing compared to the high. Crystal clear, psychoactive, and incredibly energetic, this is a strain that might just get you closer to the truth of life, the universe, and everything.

Sweet Pink Grapefruit

Spain's Alpine Seeds have been working on this Sweet Pink Grapefruit strain for 4 years now, in which time you could have had five-and-a-half kids or been in one Olympic games. The Alpine guys spent that time hard at work perfecting this inbred SPG line to make it a perfect strain for indoor or greenhouse grows.

This strain grows as a sativa-dominant plant would be expected to: with a slightly bushier structure, thanks to the indica influence. It won't grow too tall or too wild for an indoor grow, though. Greenhouse growers in mild climates will find this a particularly suitable strain for their needs, and this plant is so hardy, stable, and uniform that the crop will be beautiful. Towards the end of the 65-day flowering period your buds may even turn purple or blue, and the flowers will be so stoked with resin that you'll think you're dreaming. Expect a larger than average yield and an easy harvest.

Give these buds a nice long curing period, as you will want the sweet, tangy fruit taste to be as strong and delicious as you can make it. After the grapefruit taste subsides, the strong, intense high will make its way to your mind, spreading a relaxing stone through your body while your brain goes wandering. A great wake 'n bake strain, Sweet Pink Grapefruit is classic Swiss cannabis for the modern era brought to you by the masters at Alpine Seeds.

Alpine Seeds, Spain

Sativa-Dominant

Genetics: SPG x (SPG x SPG Breeding Line 3)

Potency: THC 19%

alpine-seeds.ch

Temple

America's Bodhi Seeds really doesn't mess about when it comes to big buds. He likes them, and he cannot lie. In fact, I'd go as far as to say that his dedication to creating absolutely massive nugs of pot borders on the psychopathic; he knows what he wants, he knows how to get it, and he'll be damned if he'll let anyone get in his way. His weapons of choice in creating this plant were the wonderful Mr. Nice's Super Silver Haze and William's Wonder, a strain which enjoys a fanbase as dedicated and passionate as the millions of pre-teen girls who seem to swarm around Justin Bieber wherever the wannabe badass decides to go. The main difference is that the William's Wonder fans are less screamy and more incredibly high.

If you're looking for a strain that will bring you everything fantastic about sativa plants with less of the headache and less of the waiting time, then Temple is for you. Sticking to a medium height, this is the sort of sativa that gives indica growers a huge sigh of relief; just when they think they're going to be scaling ladders and falling, only to swing from the branches of a 14-foot monster, they realize that this badboy is just a little shorty. It's recommended that this plant should be grown in an organic environment, especially for medical use, but it will take pretty well to whatever kind of set up you decide to use. Incredibly thin and pale green serrated leaves scream "I'M A SATIVA!" as soon as you enter the grow room, and the green hues of the emerging buds are like the icing on top of an incredibly dank-looking cake. The flowering time is also something of a surprise, as despite this plant being a card-carrying sativa, it flowers fully in only 9 or 10 weeks, and you better be ready for some serious shit to go down as soon as you flip your babies into flower. As you'll see if you glance ever so slightly to the right of these words, Temple creates colas that could make The Shard feel inadequate. A lot of my dude friends don't even like standing around these plants. It affects them, somehow.

Bodhi Seeds, USA

Sativa-Dominant

Genetics: Mr. Nice's Super Silver Haze x William's Wonder

breedbay.co.uk

cannabis-seeds-bank.co.uk

This strain can express a number of phenotypes, meaning that your high could be a more mellow social one, or you could find yourself running to the end of the street and back without being quite sure why. Whichever you end up with, you can be sure that you've got yourself some great celebratory pot, as when the citrus haze of the smoke disappears you'll notice that everyone's smiling like they're at the Mad Hatter's tea party or something. An excellent high from a stellar strain from a stellar breeder.

Terciopelo Lavanda
(Lavender Velvet)

You know that famous Seinfeld episode where Costanza says that if it were socially acceptable, he would drape himself in velvet? Well, if it were socially acceptable (and not still illegal in most places), I would drape myself in Terciopelo Lavanda, otherwise known as Lavender Velvet from Spain's Asturjaya Seeds, wearing a coat of these buds and stinking the whole place up. Seriously, I would.

A pure sativa strain from super secret genetics, this plant is a large but compact one with lots of branching. It kicks out medium-dense buds like they're going out of fashion, and each one looks as soft and stroke-able as the name might suggest. In colder climates these buds will exhibit the purple color of their name, and the huge yield of each plant makes it seem like they're already wearing coats of luxurious velvet. Indoor growers can produce between 750 and 1500 grams of bud per square yard, which is massive.

Asturjaya Seeds, Spain

Pure Sativa

Potency: THC 15%

asturjaya.es

The aroma of this plant is very floral, deep, and delicious. The smoke is sweet and fruity, and the high is all sativa: cerebral and enlightening. You'll be a happy little cat with even just a small toke on this gorgeous-tasting strain, making it a great choice for a much-needed daytime smoke.

The Onion

The USA's Cali Gold Genetics are a good source for stellar underground strains on the West Coast and beyond, and it's no wonder when they go around combining kick-ass strains like these ones as if it's easy as pie. Although their company is relatively new, the breeders behind Cali Gold have been growing, breeding, and worshipping pot for over three decades, and their love for sativas, and landrace strains in particular, is second to none. For The Onion, which I'm assuming isn't named after the satire website, these guys have combined sativa genetics from Thailand, Brazil and, most interestingly, Nigeria, to make a hybrid plant that's very sativa heavy and carries landrace traits into a plant that even inexperienced growers can love.

Although this strain is one that can be grown both indoors and out, its very nature means that outdoor growers might get more out of The Onion than indoor growers; they'll certainly come away with a larger yield. Lovers of landrace strains and pure sativas will find a lot to appreciate in this plant, and those who've had a lot of experience growing sativa-heavy hybrids will know exactly how to handle this plant. The Onion will grow tall and will be mostly thin and leggy, with sharp, dark leaves that seem to have a vendetta against anyone that walks past them; they jut out aggressively and look serrated enough to cause some decent damage! Deep down, though, this plant is a sweetheart. She is a lover of the light and has a structure that's stronger than it looks. The Onion can hold its own in a moderate to hot climate, though she won't enjoy cold snaps. At the beginning of the flowering period your Onion buds won't be very dense; they will tend towards the loose sativa style, but they will bulk up a little a few weeks into flowering. They'll also have an intriguing mix of colors; yellow green with bright pink accents. This will make your grow room look something like an 80s disco party in a sorority dorm room, but this is no bad thing. Expect a longer-than-normal flowering period thanks to the heavy sativa influence, but the wait will be well worth it.

Cali Gold Genetics, USA

Sativa-Dominant

Genetics: Thai x Nigerian x Brazilian

Potency: THC 14%

caligoldgenetics.com

I never thought I'd say this about a cannabis strain, but this plant straight up smells like onions. Actually, it smells like Vidalia onions, the type that we all have sitting in our veggie drawers and stinking up our kitchens. Once you bust them open and get them burning, the onion stink will give way to a fruity cherry smell and something else, something a little strange, at the end of your joint. This is a true pleasure to smoke.

Tom Hill's Original Haze

Grown by the wonderful Trip Seeds, based out of Chile, this strain was in fact created by Tom Hill, a breeder from Northern California who has been working out of that area for decades. Coming to Tom by way of Positronics Seeds' Original Haze from the mid 90s, this strain has been lovingly grown and improved upon to make something truly special. If, like me, you're a particular fan of Haze strains, this will be like the Holy Grail for you; a Haze that's as pure as they come. This strain could be put next to "dank" in the dictionary, but I'm not sure that Webster smokes pot. Anymore.

As a four-way hybrid of some fantastic narrow-leaf varieties from a smattering of tropical countries, namely Mexico, Colombia, Thailand, and the south of India, Haze has always been the kind of strain that makes people sit up and listen. Fans of pure sativa strains have always had a special place in their hearts for Haze, as it offers the kind of soaring, gliding high that puts you on a different level of consciousness. Unfortunately, these types of sativas are often difficult to grow, and growers in Holland or Northern California will find that Tom Hill's Original Haze will struggle to mature outdoors in both of those locations. Instead, Dutch or Cali growers are recommended to grow this strain indoors, where it will reach 8 feet with ease, so make sure you have grow rooms with some high ceilings! Rookie growers will most likely find this plant too difficult for them in any environment, as it flowers long, grows tall, and presents many challenges that may prove too much for the newbie cultivator. The flowering time will especially challenge growers, as it runs to a full 16 weeks in some cases, or 14 if you're lucky. For the best quality, you simply have to let this strain run for 3 months or more, and this can pose an issue for those with itchy harvesting fingers. Your finished Tom Hill's Original Haze buds will be wispy and look like little puffs of green cloud, being somewhat looser than indica buds but full of personality. After 3 months or more, you should pull down around 300 grams per plant.

Tom Hill, USA, grown by

Trip Seeds, Chile

Sativa-Dominant

Genetics: Positronics Original Haze

Potency: THC 13%

facebook.com/tripseeds

collectionseeds@gmail.com

That sweet but spicy Haze taste will be absolutely present in your Tom Hill's Original Haze buds; would you expect anything less? Truly, though, no one smokes Haze for the taste; it's all about that high, the kind that will pick you up, throw you through the air, and not give a fuck about where you land. A cerebral high to end all cerebral highs, this is the kind of stuff that Steve Jobs smoked before he redefined "geek cool" and made millions of hipsters part with their hard earned cash.

Trainwreck

There are some cannabis strains that you just have to love for the upfront nature of their names. Trainwreck is one of these. It does exactly what its name promises, and you're not surprised when, after getting a bit trigger happy with your favorite bong, you're left not knowing what surface you're draped over or who or what else might be in the room with you. Good thing Trainwreck warns you about that before you dive in head first. The good folks at the Humboldt Seed Organisation are also to thank, here, as their tireless dedication to producing the highest quality all-organic cannabis strains means that we, the humble tokers, get to experience such California classics as Trainwreck without having to worry that we're inhaling some horrible lung pollution in the process. We like our zombie-like highs without the additional toxins, thank you very much!

Trainwreck was born in California—in Arcata, Humboldt to be precise—and quickly became known as one of the strongest strains in the state, or, in the parlance of our times, a "real facemelter." Despite the fact that such stone-y effects are typically derived

Humboldt Seed Organisation, USA

Sativa-Dominant

Genetics: Unknown

Potency: THC 17%

humboldtseeds.co.uk

from indica strains, this is in fact a sativa-dominant, although only slightly. Whilst the stone might come from the indica side of things, the growing style certainly comes from the sativa side; this is a moderately tall plant that gets leggy if you let it and might even grow to be too big for your space if you take your eye off the ball for too long. After a respectable 9-week flowering period, or around the middle of October for outdoor growers, you can expect to bring in an enormous yield that should keep you in business for months.

I barely need to tell you what the effects of Trainwreck are like, but just in case you're a rookie toker that thinks that everyone's exaggerating when they talk about feeling like your jaw might have gone off and moved to a different county, or not being quite sure that you haven't wet your pants, let me explain. No matter what your tolerance or arrogance, this strain will sit you right down on your ass and give you a nice long lecture about what it means to be truly stoned. As this stone, however, is a psychedelic one, not only will you be slumped in a corner like you've taken an arrow to the knee, you'll also have eyes that are glazed over, your mind flying somewhere out in the stratosphere while your brain is tripping balls. In every clichéd artistic depiction of being high, there's a little of the Trainwreck experience; the colors, the confusion, the crazy euphoria. If you've never seen a Trainwreck before, you're seriously missing out.

UK Cheese

The Cheese family of cannabis strains has enjoyed the sort of enduring popularity that its namesake dairy product continues to enjoy. People can't get enough of it. Okay, they're (usually) not grating this type of Cheese on top of their shepherd's pies and all over potatoes, but they are clamoring after whatever Cheese strains that they can get their hands on. It should come as great news, then, that Spain's Shaman Genetics have been maintaining a clone of the original Exodus Cheese for over a decade, and have finally managed to give this fantastic strain a new lease on life. Using STS (silver thiosulphate) they finally got some fertile pollen from their cutting, and bred this into Skunk #1, producing what they say is the closest thing to growing from the original cut of Exodus Cheese. That's a lot of work for one plant, but everyone who loves the stinky dankness of this particular plant will know that it's totally worth it. Thank you, Shaman Genetics!

Right from the get-go, your UK Cheese seedlings will look like something special. For sativa-dominant strains, they exhibit an incredibly strong structure, and as the plants mature these thick stems will turn into a trunk that's akin to that of a pretty hefty tree. Outdoor growers will appreciate this strength in structure, as it means that your UK Cheese crop will be able to hold its own against high winds and other annoyances out in the open air. It will also grow tall outdoors, although this height can be somewhat tamed so that indoor growers don't miss out on the Cheese-growing party. This is an incredibly stable strain that will give very uniform crops, and they also tend to be very hardy; don't overdo it with any nutrients that you may be using and you'll most likely find yourself with a very easy crop to cultivate. Growers that have experience with Cheese strains will, of course, be able to get the very best out of this plant, but she won't present much of a hassle, even for relatively inexperienced growers. After flowering for 70 days indoors, your UK Cheese crop will give you around 500 grams of fantastic bud per square yard of grow space. Outdoors, harvest should be around the 20th of October, and these plants should give around 450 grams each. This is a medium yielder, but the bud is classic old school Cheese.

Shaman Genetics, Spain

Sativa-Dominant

Genetics: Exodus Cheese (Clone Only) x Skunk #1

Potency: THC 19.8%

shamangenetics.com

The large, sticky, compact buds of UK Cheese burst into that all familiar Parmesan dank that's absolutely mouthwatering even after years of tasting it, and the resulting high will have you flying right back to the glory days of Cheese. Grate some of this on your Mac 'n Cheese next time. I won't tell.

White Bhutanese

Mandala Seeds' seemingly endless stock of quality genetics from all around the globe means that we, their customers, tend to pick up some really unique strains when they're done fiddling around with them and making them all perfect. However, White Bhutanese is something for the true cannabis connoisseur; a landrace variety originally from the Wangdi Province in Bhutan. Trainspotters, get your notebooks!

An 80% sativa, this strain is one that needs to be grown outdoors or in a green-house thanks to its massive height and wild nature; after all, this strain is only one gen-eration removed from its original source. White Bhutanese enjoys warm to tropical climates and has a mercifully high resistance to mold, and growers in regions with con-stant photoperiods or especially high humidity will find that this strain is perfect for their needs. She needs a lot of nutrients, but overpruning can actually decrease landrace yields, so don't go overboard on that front; a little LST will suffice. Even in late October, when your plants are almost totally ripe, their trichomes will still be shining white rather than amber; this is a trademark of the strain.

Mandala Seeds, Spain

Sativa-Dominant

Genetics: Landrace Bhutanese from Wangdi Province

Potency: THC 12-13.8% / CBD 0.16%

mandalaseeds.com

The lemony, minty White Bhutanese smoke will give way to a creative, focused high with a good social vibe that can help sufferers of depression and anxiety. A true modern classic strain worthy of all the attention it gets!

White Diesel

Spain's Vulkania Seeds take their craft very seriously. They work with what they consider to be the cream of the genetic crop when they grow, and they don't choose their breeding stock lightly. They also know to give credit where credit is due, so this strain is dedicated to Vulkania Seeds founder El Aguila—and after you've had a taste of this fantastic White Diesel, you'll be bowing down and offering your gratitude to the man known as "The Eagle" as well. A cross between NYC Diesel and a White Widow plant, this at first may not seem like anything out of the ordinary, but when you dig a little deeper into the genetic family tree you realize that this is going to be one helluva strain.

The NYC Diesel plant used in this strain is actually from 2006; the mother of the original V2.0, this strain is memorably fantastic for its many sought-after traits which have led to it being regarded as prime Diesel breeding stock. The other parent plant is a White Widow from 2004, which also became the mother of the famous White Eva strain. By combining these two plants, Vulkania have sired a sativa-dominant strain that leans more towards NYC Diesel on the structural side but has more of a White Widow high. Although White Diesel is only a medium tall plant, it should be allowed to grow to its full potential for the very best results. It is recommended that this plant be grown indoors, although it can also be cultivated outdoors to good effect. Indoor growers will find that the best set up is to grow under at least 600 watts of HPS lighting, and the breeders recommend feeding often and heavy to get the best yield. This strain gives good clones which will take root quickly. It has a 14 day vegetative period and towards the end of the 55 day flowering period this crop will enjoy rich fertilizer (high in potassium and phosphorus) to help stack more compact buds and enhance their final flavor. Outdoors, White Diesel can grow to 7 feet in height, and the breeders recommend growing in a good-quality, well-aerated soil with a high level of organic matter. Use pots no less than 3 gallons, and expect to harvest around the second week of October. While indoor growers will take down around 600 grams per square yard of grow space, outdoor growers can take down about 850 grams per plant. This is a definite heavy yielder!

Gorgeous white buds with a fluffy feel will burst into a riot of White Widow and fuel-like flavors that express both tastes of the parent plants. The White Diesel high is a calm, relaxing one, but it also gives a great deal of mood enhancement.

Vulkania Seeds, Spain

Sativa-Dominant

Genetics: NYC Diesel x White Widow

Potency: THC 20%

vulkaniaseeds.es

Wild Thailand

Sativa aficionados are an interesting bunch, and if you've ever met a true trainspotter-style sativa lover, you'll have known it instantly. Not only do they have the tweaking exuberance of someone who's been toking on energy-giving joints all day long and the vaguely glassy-eyed stare of someone who's sort of tripping, but they can hear a sativa reference from 100 yards and will take literally any opportunity to start extolling the virtues of a 14-foot landrace from Hawaii. If you think you might have met a sativa lover but you're not quite sure, sneak up to them quietly and when you're in range, whisper "Wild Thailand" under your breath. Non-sativa divas will simply carry on what they're doing. Actual sativa divas will turn on a dime, beam like kids at Christmas, and start chewing your ear off about this World of Seeds strain from the Ko Chang archipelago in Thailand.

You really can't blame them: this is one hell of a plant. A pure Thai sativa, Wild Thailand is apparently highly appreciated by growers in her native land, who face extreme punishment every day of their lives thanks to Thailand's archaic penal system and the extreme prejudice with which the police apply those anti-cannabis rules. Despite this, Wild Thailand is smuggled in and out of Bangkok regularly, which should give you some indication of how highly her lineage is prized inside and outside the country. A very tall plant with almost uncontrollable growth, Wild Thailand is made to grow in the great outdoors, and will flourish best when planted with plenty of room for her roots to spread.

World of Seeds, Spain

Pure Sativa

Genetics: Landrace Ko Chang Thai

Potency: THC 22.3%

worldofseeds.eu

She can, however, be grown indoors, too, but she'll still command a lot of room and attention. She's very resistant to mold, moderately resistant to pests, and tends to forgive you if you get carried away with the watering, although you should never take that for granted. A light breeze in the grow room will help her stems grow thick rather than spindly, which will also help her to support her massive yields in the later stages of flowering. You'll most definitely need to stake and train her. Expect 300 grams from an indoor plant and up to 500 grams from an outdoor one.

Your finished Wild Thailand buds will look and smell like something truly special; the odor will be almost overbearing, and once you break those nugs open and vaporize or smoke them, you'll find that the taste hits just the same. That spicy, Haze-y Asian taste of pure sativas is more than abundant here, and the spectacularly euphoric high will take your feelings and catapult them into the sky. Wild Thailand will turn you into a true sativa-spotter if you're not too careful!

Y Griega

Y Griega is a fascinating and very strong sativa-dominant strain from Spain's Medical Seeds Company, who you may not have heard of but who you should be writing down for future reference as their strains are something to behold. Y Griega, which was the previous name for the Spanish letter "y" before they decided to just call it "ye" (educational standards continue to fall), is a sativa-dominant hybrid of Kali Mist and Amnesia, two of the most popular sativas of all time. The Haze grandparent strain comes through strongly in this plant, meaning that Haze fans will really appreciate this plant, especially if they're indoor growers. As with all strains created by Medical Seeds Company, Y Griega makes excellent hash and oil.

I've spoken before about the hybrid revolution that brought sativa growing to indoor growers, but it can only truly be appreciated in plants like this that have a hell of a lot of Haze influence, as only a couple of decades ago when indoor growing was king, no one would have ever hoped that they could grow Haze plants indoors.

Medical Seeds Co, Spain

Sativa-Dominant

Genetics: Kali Mist x Amnesia

Potency: THC 27.12%

medicalseeds.net

As it stands, Y Griega can reach up to 11 feet outdoors, but those growing in confined spaces will find that through Low Stress Training and various other methods, this can be a fine strain to grow indoors. The breeders highly recommend growing in a ScrOG set up, as this makes the vigor of this strain more easily manageable. Regardless of your grow set up, Y Griega will start out its life much like the universe, with a huge surge of power and dramatic force. If you're looking to keep it to 6 feet or under, be sure to force flowering when the plant is at half that height or even smaller; this will ensure that it doesn't get too out of control. There isn't an inch of Y Griega stem that's not covered in buds by the end of the 90 day flowering period, and since these nugs are all covered in thick white hair, your grow room will look like a white Christmas. Outdoors, look to harvest around the beginning of November, and you should be able to bring in a yield of around 550 grams per plant. Indoors, 550 grams is what you'll get from a square yard of grow space using the ScrOG method. Not too shabby at all!

This classic Haze scent will send your expectations for this strain soaring, and then the high will throw you right up in the air to super smash them into a million pieces. A bolt of energy and you're gone, only to float down to earth in a relaxing bubble a few hours later. Perfection.

Index

Index

Index

Index